D1607736

# ESCAPE FROM STRESS
*How to Stop Killing Yourself*

# ESCAPE
# FROM STRESS

## How to Stop Killing Yourself

*by Kenneth Lamott*

*G. P. Putnam's Sons, New York*

PRINTED IN THE UNITED STATES OF AMERICA

For
Ben Chamberlain,
who survived,
and
Howard Nelson,
who didn't

# Contents

# Foreword

IN SPITE of the great and well-publicized victories that have been won by biomedical scientists and brilliant clinicians, the problem of survival in the face of mounting stress appears to be getting progressively worse.

This book grew out of a succession of somber events that have occurred around me during the past few years. During this time a number of friends of mine, all in their late forties and early fifties, cracked up under the stresses of their lives.

Two committed suicide. Another suffered several heart attacks. Still another friend tried to kill himself by washing down a bottle of sleeping pills with a pint of vodka, but his outraged stomach rejected the mixture. One more is recovering from a succession of physical disasters, including a heart attack and a stroke, and will never regain his full vigor, which was considerable.

I could go on with other personal disasters, but the message is clear. We are suffering from a veritable epidemic, a plague of stress-induced disease and disorders that cripple and kill. Heart attacks, strokes, and suicide are only the most visible entries in a long and melancholy catalogue. Nor are men who are passing through middle age the only people at risk. The rise of the stress diseases among young and middle-aged women—particularly those working in positions of responsibility—is dramatic and disheartening. The problem of survival is real and involves everybody.

My concern for my own continued survival was the principal private motive that led me to write this book. Circumstances in the great world outside were also conducive to an enterprise of this sort. I was encouraged to observe that the general intellectual climate of our time is becoming more receptive to the notion that not everything that is real can yet be described with the present resources of science.

One of the worst-kept secrets of our so-called scientific age is that, particularly when we come to the behavior of human beings, nonscience sometimes works as successfully—and often more successfully—than does hard science. The yogi *does* control the beating of his heart. People suffering from real diseases *are* sometimes cured by faith healers. The firewalker *does* walk unhurt over glowing coals. The Christian Scientist *doesn't* necessarily die any earlier than does the doctor's daughter. The patient under acupuncture *does* smile while his gallbladder is being removed. Information *does* pass between people in ways that science cannot describe.

This is not to say that scientists may not someday (perhaps tomorrow) account for each of these phenomena in a purely mechanistic manner. They have not done so yet. But they are now moving in directions that were, by a sort of unspoken agreement, closed to them before. As Dr. Sydney G. Margolin of the University of Colorado medical school remarked to me, "The young people's interest in drugs and hallucinogens and so on has opened up to curious scientists the opportunity to study all sorts of things. The results are now very much in the foreground."

As I went on with my research, my attention became focused on two particular points. First, as I reviewed the medical and biological literature on stress and its consequences, it quickly became clear that an increasing number of diseases and disorders have been found to be related to stress. Among these conditions are not only heart disease, peptic ulcers, high blood pressure, and headaches but also skin disorders, arthritis, asthma, cardiac arrhythmias, colitis, diarrhea, and even cancer—and this is by no means an inclusive list. Furthermore, a substantial argument can be made that we are struck down by the infectious diseases only when we are in a state of stress.

The second point on which my interest became focused was the observation that at a number of laboratories across the country (from Harvard's medical school to Stanford's department of psychology) reputable and imaginative investigators are working on research projects that bear on the problem of stress and that may lead us to adopt an entirely different working relationship with our bodies.

The physiological effects produced by yogis and Zen masters have been examined with sensitive laboratory equipment and found to be measurable. The feats of Indian fakirs —such as driving needles through their bodies—have been replicated in the laboratory. Faith healers have participated in laboratory experiments and appeared in seminars with orthodox medical men.

A lively debate is going on over the real nature of hypnosis, even as it is being applied to an increasing range of clinical conditions. Acupuncture has become a seven-day wonder. Finally, the electronics revolution that followed World War II has made possible the development of instruments that have opened up an entirely new field of learning—the learning of control over such internal processes as heartbeat, blood pressure, and the electrical waves produced by our brains.

Out of all this varied scientific activity has come the clear suggestion that we may well be on the way to finding some usable answers to the problem of stress. We have already come a longer way than most people know.

Effective techniques each of us can use do lie at hand to help us relieve the stress in our lives and promote psychological and physiological equilibrium. This in turn gives us the means to live more robust and longer lives.

There is a great hunger for instruction of this sort. At the Stanford hypnosis laboratory I was told by the director, Dr. Ernest R. Hilgard, "We'd be simply overwhelmed if we opened the doors to people who need help, particularly if they're in pain."

Hypnosis, faith healing, yoga, and the like have always provided fertile fields for the quack and the charlatan. I have accordingly drawn my witnesses from the ranks of people who have earned such evidence of seriousness as the MD or PhD degrees.

Among those who contributed personally to my understanding of these matters are (alphabetically) Dr. Theodore Xenophon Barber of the Medfield State Hospital, near Boston; Dr. Thomas Budzynski of the University of Colorado Medical School; Dr. David B. Cheek, an obstetrician and gynecologist practicing in San Francisco; Dr. Elmer Green and Mrs. Alyce Green of the Menninger Foundation, who conducted a landmark seminar on these topics; Dr. Hilgard of Stanford; Dr. Joe (not Joseph) Kamiya of the Langley Porter Neuropsychiatric Institute; Dr. Demetri Kanallakos of the Stanford Research Institute; Dr. Margolin of Colorado; Dr. Neal Miller of the Rockefeller University; and Dr. Johann Stoyva, also of the University of Colorado.

A word remains to be said about the relationship between the matters treated in this book and conventional scientific medicine. I am not by any means hostile to scientific medicine—in fact, I have earned part of my living for many years as a planning consultant to medical schools. I do not myself see any insoluble conflict between the stress theory of disease and accepted medical practice. The stress-relieving techniques that will be described should be looked on as supplements rather than substitutes for conventional treatment.

Finally, I must add a word of caution to the reader who follows the instructions given later in this book for meditation, self-hypnosis, and autogenic training. Investigators in these fields have reported that some individuals are afflicted with feelings of depression and loneliness after attempting these practices. Any hint of depression, of course, is a strong indication that one should stop. In any case, if one has the opportunity to learn these practices under supervision, the road will be both shorter and smoother.

# Part I
## THE RAVAGES OF STRESS

# 1

# The Stress of Life

## STRESS AND DISEASE

THE IDEA that the stress of life can cause real bodily disease, that it is responsible for most physical suffering and that it can kill as surely as poison can kill, is both ancient and revolutionary.

In order to understand the power of this idea we must divest ourselves of the common notions that psychosomatic disease is somehow not real and that its sufferers are neurotics who attract attention or escape from their personal problems by falling victim to imaginary ailments. Neurotic they may be (are we not all to some extent neurotic?), but their illnesses are mortally real.

The stress-induced heart attack or bleeding ulcer or high blood pressure or cancer kills its victim as thoroughly as if he were crushed to death in an automobile accident. Psychosomatic disease is real—and in fact there is a small minority of medical men who believe all disease is psychosomatic.

This idea has been with us through the centuries, sometimes buried and sometimes highly visible. In the twentieth century it has emerged in the work of such medical pioneers as H. Flanders Dunbar, Franz Alexander, Harold G. Wolff, and Hans Selye—all of them highly respected physicians and teachers.

In the wake of these trailblazers the idea that stress can generate not only psychological disorders but also bodily dis-

15

eases has fastened itself on the minds of an increasingly large number of practicing physicians and laboratory investigators. It has pushed the frontiers of medicine in a direction diametrically opposed to the discovery of more vaccines, wonder drugs and miracle operations.

It has raised the possibility that our greatest medical need may not be the discovery of new medicines or operative procedures but the discovery of a new view of life and of new devices to cope with the strain of adjusting to the inevitable changes in our personal lives. That is what this book is about.

It is highly ironic that as these medical pioneers lead us in this new direction, we come face to face with some figures that scientific medicine thought it had left behind in the mists of history—the faith healer, the yogi, the pulse diagnostician, the acupuncturist, the mesmerist, the medicine man. All the practitioners of nonscientific medicine and their undoubted successes in healing must now be viewed from a different perspective. They are not necessarily charlatans. They are often healers—and, for that matter, even charlatans have been known to heal.

An amusing and revealing sidelight on the relations between scientific practitioners and faith healers was offered at a medical school conference at which Dr. Eugene A. Stead, Jr., who teaches medicine at Duke, declared wryly, "I happen to come from the Bible Belt, as does Oral Roberts, and Oral and I have been competing in the practice of medicine for a good many years. He wins some and I win some. It is interesting that sometimes I am so paralyzed by the pathology that I cannot really believe the patient can function. Oral, not knowing the pathology, may end up with a very good functional result. When the patient asks me about it, I just say Oral was smarter than I."

This entertaining story has hidden in it the seed of a great and pervasive revolution in the prevention and treatment of illness. As the theory of stress becomes more widely understood, it will bring about changes in our understanding of disease that may be even more farreaching in their effects than were the consequences of the revolution that followed the work of Pasteur and Koch.

Whether emotional or physical, natural or man-made, public or private, stress exerts an influence on our lives that has yet to be measured in its entirety. Stress, more than any other factor (except perhaps our genetic heritage), determines the point at which we find ourselves sliding down the slope from health to disease. Stress is not unique to Americans, but given our way of living, one would not be far off to call it the "American disease."

It has been demonstrated many times that we are infected all of the time with a host of organisms, some of them potentially dangerous, which we tolerate without harm until a stressful event tips the balance. Disease, in this view, is a consequence of failing to adapt to stress.

Some physicians and biologists believe that all diseases are triggered by stress. Many more believe that all (or at least most) diseases have a stress component. Among diseases in which a stress component has been identified are major killers and minor annoyances—heart disease and bleeding gums, high blood pressure and hay fever, cancer and the common cold.

Other scientists agree with Hans Selye that each of us possesses only a fixed store of vitality on which we can draw to respond to stressful happenings. This store of vital energy can never be replenished. It can only be used up. When we fail to mobilize our vital energy effectively, we fall sick. When our total store of vitality runs low, we show the signs of aging. When our store of vitality is used up, we die.

Before we go on, there is a related matter that we must understand, and this is that we are all subject to the ravages of stress. Each of us would like to believe that succumbing to a stress-induced disease is a weakness of *other* people. Nothing could be less true. Resistance varies from person to person, but there comes a point at which each one of us will succumb.

It is, of course, also true that a stress that may be im-

mediately harmful to one person may act as a stimulating
challenge to another. But as stress increases, the challenge at
last becomes insurmountable and in the end crushing.
Under sufficient force, even the strongest bone will break.

It is always tempting to argue that the modern world is a
uniquely difficult place in which to live and that we are
obliged to endure stressors with which our ancestors never
had to cope. While there is some truth here, there is also
nonsense.

Although our modern industrialized world exposes us to a
different collection of stressors than were found in a world
that supported itself by farming, anybody who is familiar
with the history and imaginative literature of the past three
thousand years is not likely to make the mistake of picturing
our forefathers living in a bucolic world full of peace and
happiness.

The stressors that affect the greatest number of lives are
essentially the same in any period, whether it is the period of
the Roman Empire, the Hundred Years War or the Industrial Revolution. Change in one's personal circumstances is
the most common and most powerful stressor.

An example is found in the experience of motherhood.
One of the greatest life changes is found in the birth of a
woman's first child. Not only does the style of her daily life
change, but her very identity changes. She is now a mother,
with all the real and sentimental attributes of that state.

In recent years Dr. John C. Cassel of the University of
North Carolina has been studying the effects of stress on
first-time mothers who were experiencing stressful social
readjustments. He found that there was a 30 percent chance
of complications during childbirth if they were well-loved
and supported during these readjustments—a figure high
enough to be alarming in itself. But the chance of complications leaped threefold, to 90 percent, if the young mothers-
to-be received little warm support from their husbands and
relatives.

In a related study Dr. Cassel also discovered that divorced men have a death rate three to five times as high as married men of the same age. There are marked changes in the hormone levels of people who have been deprived of warm social approval, he explained, leaving them more vulnerable to disease.

"Generalized susceptibility also explains why the parts of the United States which have the highest heart disease rates (all large cities) also have the highest rates for cancer, strokes, and so on," Cassel said. He concluded, somewhat chillingly, "They have a susceptibility to dying."

The next great advance in the healing arts will be a frontal assault on the problem of stress. We need to know much more about the relationship of stress to health and disease. We need to know if particular stresses favor particular diseases or if stress is general and our particular response is determined by our immediate circumstances and our genetic heritage. We need to know how to handle stress as a public-health problem and to discover how to reduce the occurrence of stress disease in entire populations. (The incidence of hypertension—or high blood pressure—among black residents of our inner cities is a case in point.) There are many other related problems to which we do not now have the answers.

We are, however, beginning to understand that ancient methods of relieving stress and promoting tranquility have been shown in the laboratory to bring about desirable changes in some of the vital functions of our bodies. Practitioners of yoga and Zen have shown scientific investigators that they can cause a wide range of changes in such basic functions as breathing, heart rate, blood pressure, and the electrical activity of the brain.

The accumulating evidence that this control is real —evidence that comes from some of our most respected medical schools—is the basis for our exploration in this book of several techniques for relieving stress. We will learn ·to

reduce our individual levels of stress through a yogic breathing exercise, through meditation, through hypnosis,
through autogenic training, and through biofeedback.

These exercises will help us strengthen our defenses
against the stress that unavoidably enters into each of our
lives. They will not cure disease. They will merely improve
the odds in favor of a healthier and longer life.

But first let us explore some recent investigations into the
nature of stress and the extent of its ravages.

## STRESS AND SURVIVAL

During the course of history men have interpreted the
coming of illness in a variety of ways. To the ancient Jews the
sufferer was a guilty person atoning for his sin. To the
Greeks illness was a great evil, an imperfection in the ideal
state. Only with the coming of Christianity was the patient
delivered from odium (as the great medical historian Henry
E. Segrist once put it) and the act of healing given a signifi-
cance not far behind the salvation of the soul.

We ourselves recognize that some diseases—cirrhosis of
the liver, for example—are brought on by destructive ways
of life. By and large, however, we believe that sickness is
neither punishment nor imperfection but an accidental
event, an almost random striking down by an external agent,
such as a germ or a virus.

When we set out to conquer a disease—as we are now
trying to conquer cancer—we encourage men in white coats
to track down the disease-causing agent, just as they have
done successfully in the cases of malaria or typhoid. As René
Dubos has observed ironically, "Whatever the nature of the
disease, the important task—so at least is the well-nigh universal belief—is to discover some magic bullet capable of
reaching and destroying the responsible demon within the
body of the patient."

Even after we give all honor to the men in white we also
know that the germ, virus, or other microscopic demon does

not cause the disease. We are all infected all of the time with a wide variety of microorganisms. Some of these bacilli, streptococci, pneumococci, and staphylococci are extremely virulent, but not all of us become sick. It is not beyond possibility that the great mass of human beings harbor without ill effects a virus that can produce cancer, but that the cancer strikes only when external or internal events change the relationship between the virus and its host.

A classic demonstration of the natural immunity of a healthy, unstressed person was performed almost a hundred years ago by the German biochemist Max von Pettenkofer, who drank a massive dose of the organism that causes cholera. Neither he—nor the members of his staff who followed his bold example—contracted anything worse than a mild diarrhea.

The explanation is neat, fascinating, and casts a sharp light on the interrelatedness of stress and physiology. The cholera bacillus cannot infect man until it reaches his small intestine. It is killed by the acidity of the normal stomach and never reaches the intestine of an unstressed and otherwise healthy person. If stress or another disease has caused the acidity of the stomach to change, however, the bacillus passes through to the intestine, and the unfortunate human host succumbs to massive diarrhea, vomiting, dehydration, and very likely dies.

This is apparently why, during a cholera epidemic, young children will often survive, while their parents, who are much more aware of the dangers around them, will die. One could say that they had been killed by their fear.

A more homely example is contained in a study by Drs. Lawrence E. Hinkle and William N. Christensen, who followed the incidence of "Asian flu" among twenty-four women during the course of a flu season. Samples of blood serum were examined periodically for the presence of the flu virus.

It turned out that there was little correlation between the presence of the virus and the incidence of flu. The women most heavily infected with the virus often remained healthy, while those who succumbed often showed less infection.

The connection the researchers did find was not between the virus and the disease but between emotional stress and the disease. The women who succumbed were precisely those who had undergone some painful or at least disagreeable emotional experience.

Not far from these findings is the common observation that we often come down with a cold and take to our beds when we are threatened with an unpleasant confrontation. Even our language gives us away. We "catch" cold (or the flu or measles) just as we catch a ball or catch a plane. The verb is transitive, and it describes a purposeful action.

In both short-lasting, common illnesses and in more serious diseases, our attitude toward the disease itself is a complicated one. We unconsciously and irrationally inflict the disease on ourselves when some degree of suffering is preferable to the other alternatives open to us. As Freud and other acute observers both before and after his time have noted, sickness and disability are often chosen over health and activity.

There are ancient echoes in our understanding that the onset of disease is often accompanied by (and may be connected with) feelings of sin, guilt, inferiority, and unworthiness. Although the precise workings of cause and effect are not yet clear to us, we stand today at the brink of an entirely new concept of health and disease, a concept that does not deny the great accomplishments of the scientific era of medicine but that reconsiders and reframes these accomplishments in terms of ideas that are older than Pasteur and Koch.

It is not always true that human progress invariably swings back and forth like a pendulum, but it is often a useful analogy. We have gone about as far as we can in the perfection of the physical-chemical model of disease. We are swinging back toward the long-understood truth that disease involves a breakdown in the victim's harmony with his internal and external environments. Disease is not caused by a germ but by a change in our relationship to the germ.

We are going back to an idea that was expressed elegantly in the Chinese doctrine of the harmony of yin and yang, and that showed itself in different garb in the American Indian's belief that he must remain in harmony with nature.

We are seeing the pendulum swing away from Pasteur and toward his friend Claude Bernard, the great French physiologist.

*"La fixité du milieu intérieur est la condition essentielle de la vie libre,"* Bernard wrote. [The constancy of the internal milieu is the essential condition of free life.] All living things survive in a state of health so long as they can maintain a precise balance in the physical and chemical functioning of their bodies.

The great Pasteur himself became convinced of the overriding importance of the *milieu intérieur.* His dying words are reported to have been, "Bernard was right. The microbe is nothing, the terrain is everything."

Bernard's discovery (or rediscovery) of the principle that harmony means health was carried further by the physiologist Walter B. Cannon of Harvard, who forty years ago described the body's powerful tendency to correct an imbalance. The operation of this exquisite mechanism Cannon called homeostasis, which he described in the title of his great book as the "wisdom of the body."

This new-old view of health and disease, then, is that they are not merely personal matters between microorganisms and human beings but are matters that may involve an entire spectrum of other relationships, including relationships with one's spouse, employer, children, neighbors, and spiritual and medical advisers.

Furthermore, one's health may be affected in a very real way by the newspapers one reads, the television shows one watches, and the conversations one has, as well as by the air one breathes, the water one drinks, and the food one eats. Wars and rumors of wars affect the health of people far from the battlefield. Violence breeds disease.

The assassination of President Kennedy set off a veritable epidemic of minor disorders. Eighty-nine percent of the people interviewed by the National Opinion Research Center during the week after the murder reported they had lost their appetites or had headaches or upset stomachs or had been unable to sleep or had been afflicted by general nervousness. We can only speculate on the number of people who suffered more serious and lasting damage.

It is not at all facetious to suggest that the Watergate scandal may be found to be responsible for a change in the incidence of some diseases—and not confined to Mr. Nixon's bouts with viral pneumonia and phlebitis.

By *stress*, then, we mean not just the well-publicized "executive stress" experienced by the ambitious, upward-striving man who is running too hard, but the stress that is produced in anybody whenever there is a significant disruption of his environment.

The disruption may come from within, in the shape of a deeply buried psychic wound that works its way to the surface and makes it impossible for the person to live at peace with himself. More likely it comes from outside, from pressures in the family, working, or social worlds. Even the most benign change in one's life—going on vacation or getting a better job—adds to the total stress that may set off a disease.

Scientific workers interested in the relationship between stress and disease generally follow the lead of Cannon and Dr. Hans Selye of the University of Montreal, one of the great leaders in the study of stress. According to their view of the matter, we become victims of biologically based response called the fight-or-flight reaction whenever we are exposed to a stressor, whether it is physical or psychological.

The fight-or-flight reaction was established as a survival mechanism during the long ages of the evolutionary process. When we are faced with a threat, powerful hormones are released into the bloodstream, and the sympathetic division of the autonomic nervous system prepares the body for instant action—whether it is fight or flight.

The autonomic nervous system received its name because in many respects it operates autonomously or independently of conscious thought. It is the branch of the central nervous system that controls the organs and glands of our bodies rather than the muscles with which we consciously cause our bodies to move. The autonomic system regulates the beating of our hearts, the activities of our endocrine glands, the temperature of our skin.

The autonomic system consists of two exquisitely balanced parts, which are called its sympathetic and parasympathetic branches. The sympathetic branch is stimulated by stress. It is responsible for mobilizing the body for action, and for all the familiar symptoms of surprise and fear, such as rapid heartbeat, sweaty palms, and cold skin. The parasympathetic system acts in precisely the opposite way, slowing the heart, drying the palm, and warming the skin.

Virtually all our vital organs are connected to both systems. If we are to survive, our bodies must maintain a delicate balance, being prepared when necessary to respond to the commands of the sympathetic branch to take instant action, but not allowing the sympathetic system to become dominant and keep us in a constant state of inappropriate vigilance. Many of the survival mechanisms we will explore are believed to work because they reinforce the calming action of the parasympathetic system.

We react to sudden stress—such as a near accident on the highway—through the following train of events:

The car that is approaching us at high speed in the wrong lane is perceived by our eyes. This information is transmitted to the brain. The sympathetic branch of the autonomic system goes into action. That part of the brain called the hypothalamus (which, ironically, is also one of the so-called pleasure centers) stimulates the pituitary gland. The pituitary releases the hormone ACTH into the bloodstream. The

ACTH travels in the blood from the pituitary, which is at the base of the brain, to the adrenals, above the kidneys.

The adrenal glands then flood the bloodstream with adrenalin, cortisone, and other "stress hormones." These travel through the bloodstream, causing a variety of useful physical effects: The pupils of our eyes become larger. Our hearing becomes sharper. Muscle tone improves. There is a change in the electrical activity of the brain. The palms of our hands sweat. Blood rushes to our head. Our fingers and toes grow cold. Our heart rate increases. We breathe faster. We swerve out of the way of the approaching car.

The accident is averted, but our body pays a price for each incident of this sort.

The fight-or-flight reaction is still essential to survival in warfare, in contact sports, and in the daily horror of driving the freeways. Yet all too often the stressor may be only our supervisor asking if we have finished drafting a report or our spouse asking what time we will be home. A reaction that was once a lifesaver in a world of hunters and warriors has become a crippler and killer in a world for which it is no longer appropriate.

When we take thought for our own survival, our central and most urgent problem is that of preserving the stability of the *milieu intérieur* in the face of all the assaults that are constantly being made on it. Medical men and biologists who have become convinced of the overriding importance of stress in changing health into disease have described the problem from various points of view with their personal vocabularies but with a common message.

The late Dr. Harold G. Wolff, a pioneer in stress studies, described health as a condition that exists so long as basic human needs, including the interpersonal and esthetic needs, are satisfied and opportunities are provided for the expression of fundamental human proclivities.

Hans Selye has advised us of the importance of arranging our lives so that we do not draw unnecessarily on an irreplaceable store of vital energy that is used when we have to cope with stress.

René Dubos of the Rockefeller University has written that effective steps in preventing disease may come from a revolt against the inadequacies of the modern world and from the search for a formula of life closer to the natural propensities of man.

Dr. John C. Cassel has shown a relationship between health and love and illness and the lack of love.

Dr. Andrew Weil has argued that all disease is psychosomatic and is made possible by the breakdown of communication between the conscious and unconscious minds.

Whatever the words may be, the common thought here is an extraordinarily powerful one: Disease is not caused by a demon. The most effective way of preventing disease is to address oneself directly to keeping one's environment stable in the face of all the stressors that threaten its disruption.

## STRESS AND NATURE

Nature was the first stressor.

Extreme cold, extreme heat, wind, drought, rain, snow, sleet, and storms on land and sea stressed primitive man, who cowered in his cave or under a roof of boughs. The forces of nature continue to stress us, striking us on one side with their direct physical effects and on the other side with fear and dread.

Because these are natural forces, we tend to accept their consequences as inescapable. We "catch cold," we believe, after we have become chilled. We become limp and irritable when a heat wave goes on and on. We become depressed by prolonged rains. We get "cabin fever" when we are snowbound. But the effect of these stressors on the machinery of our bodies is much more complex and subtle than it seems at first and cannot be charged to simple fatigue and monotony.

Two thousand years ago, Shih Huang Ti, who was known as "the First Emperor," asked his physician, "Does not the troublesome wind cause illness?"

The physician Ch'i Po answered, "The troublesome wind

affects, as a rule, the place beneath the lungs, bringing about illness in this place."

Ch'i Po's observation is still true.

The troublesome wind that is called the Santa Ana in Southern California, the *hamsin* in the Arab countries, the *Föhn* in Germany, Switzerland, and Austria, and the *mistral* in France, gives us a splendid example of the interrelatedness of emotional and physical equilibrium.

Whatever the language and wherever the place, troublesome winds bring depression, headache, breathing troubles, and outbreaks of violent behavior. In Israel this stressful wind, which is called the *sharav*, is known to cause unpleasant symptoms among at least half the population of Jerusalem. At the Hebrew University there a most extraordinary series of investigations demonstrated that the effects of the wind from the desert are both emotional and physiological.

Professor F. G. Shulman and his colleagues went about their study by analyzing the urine of some four hundred persons in Jerusalem and in the desert. They found that in addition to the general sense of irritation and raw nerves brought about by the *sharav*, there were also physiological effects that could be demonstrated in the laboratory.

Histamine was found in the urine of some sufferers from the *sharav*. Their tolerance to the hot wind was increased by giving them drugs that depressed the activity of the thyroid glands, which control the production of histamine. In other people the fatigue, apathy, and general weakness that comes with the *sharav* was found to be due to insufficient adrenalin. They were relieved of their symptoms when they took a substance called monoamine oxidase, which helps the body make better use of its adrenalin.

But the most extraordinary physiological effect was found to be an increase of the serotonin in the blood. (Serotonin acts to constrict the blood vessels and contract the muscles.) The increase of serotonin, which was held responsible for tension, irritability, headaches, and vomiting, was found to be linked to an excess of positive ions in the hot, dry wind. (An ion is an atom that holds an electrical charge.) When sufferers were either given medication that reduced the production of serotonin or kept in atmospheres where the positive ion count had been reduced electrically, their symptoms, too, were relieved.

Old Ch'i Po would not have understood the scientific explanations, but the message would not have surprised him. Physical stress produces emotional reactions; emotional stress produces physical reactions. Whether we talk of the balance of serotonin in the blood or of the harmony of yin and yang is perhaps not so very important.

A phenomenon of nature much more basic than the desert wind is the alternation of night and day, of light and darkness. Several years ago the author Joseph Wechsberg traveled to the Norwegian city of Trømso, the world's northernmost city of any size, where for fifty-one days in the winter the sun doesn't rise above the horizon. The local people told Wechsberg that paradoxically they found it almost impossible to sleep during the twenty-four-hour darkness, or *mørketiden*. Their usual habits were disrupted, and they would spend the nights reading or following hobbies, sleeping for only very short periods.

Dr. Karl Hartviksen, a physician, commented on another paradox: People were more seriously affected by the *mørketiden* after it was over rather than during the darkness itself.

"Men can take a lot of stress," Dr. Hartviksen said, "but they seem to break after the period of stress has ended. In our psychiatric wards, springtime, after the end of *mørketiden*, is the busiest period."

These distressing effects are surely due to a disruption of the sufferers' circadian rhythm, which, we are now beginning to understand, has a profound effect on our health.

"Circadian" is derived from the Latin words *circa* (about) and *diem* (day). Circadian rhythms are the regular and recurring physiological changes our bodies undergo during a cycle of about twenty-four hours. They are the tidal movements of the body and are deeply implanted in all living things.

As Gay Gaer Luce has pointed out in her fascinating

book *Biological Rhythms in Human and Animal Physiology,* there are hours during the day when each of us has periods of greatest strength and greatest weakness, periods when we survive stress easily or when we succumb easily, periods when we tend to fall ill and periods when we appear to be immune.

Animal experiments have shown that a stressor that kills at one time of day will be harmless at another.

Only 6 percent of a group of rats were killed by a dose of amphetamine given at the end of their daily activity cycle. But 78 percent died when an identical amount of the drug was administered in the middle of the cycle.

An anesthetic (halothane) given to laboratory mice killed 5 percent of them at one time of day and 76 percent at another.

Doses of x-rays that merely made animals sick during the day killed the animals when they were exposed to the radiation at night.

Mice were injected with doses of alcohol equivalent to about a quart of vodka for a man. If the alcohol was given while they were waking up, about 60 percent died. If the alcohol was given at the beginning of their rest period, only 12 percent died.

Animal experiments are based on the proposition that what is true of one species is often true of another. Human beings also vary in their vulnerability to stressors during the course of their daily activity cycle. This is a matter of common experience, for we are all aware that an irritant that will merely annoy us on one occasion will set off an anger storm at another. The influence of the circadian rhythm may, however, go far beyond this, for there is growing evidence that not only our health but our survival itself may be linked to its influence.

The mechanism is thought to operate in two ways:

First, disease or disorder may strike when our resistance is at its daily low—at the point of the circadian rhythm when we

are most vulnerable to emotional stress, to poisons, to infection, and to pain.

Secondly, there may be a disruption of the circadian rhythm itself, a stretching or compressing or twisting of the cycle. This has been shown experimentally to produce symptoms of psychological and physical disorder. The extent to which the disruption of the circadian rhythm acts as a stressor to produce psychosomatic illness is a subtle and serious problem we are just beginning to understand.

Curt Richter of Johns Hopkins has speculated that the various parts of our bodily machinery have particular rhythms or cycles of their own. Normally these cycles are out of phase, and the body as a whole remains relatively constant. But sometimes a stressor will jar the system so that some of these subcycles fall into the same pattern. Their effects then become exaggerated and we perceive a waxing and waning that we call symptoms of distress.

It is clearly the natural condition of man to live in a state of stress. Even more destructive than the stresses of nature, however, are the multitudinous stresses man creates for himself.

## STRESS AND MAN

During the history of the civilized world a substantial part of the male population has been given the usually unwelcome opportunity to test itself against the stress of extreme situations by taking part in warfare. In modern times the effects of prolonged battlefield stress were described and studied in World War I as "shell shock" and in World War II as "combat fatigue."

Whatever it is called, combat stress follows a course of increasing disablement, beginning with irritability and progressing to depression, apathy, and withdrawal. The end is typically a complete paralysis of the mind and the will.

An emotionally stable soldier endures combat stress only a

little better than the neurotic soldier. The already neurotic soldier broke down in World War II after thirty days in front-line combat; the healthy soldier broke down after thirty-six. Only the length of time is different, and not by much, for as the stressor becomes more severe, the predisposing factors become less and less important. In the end everybody breaks down.

The civilian experiences of war are equally destructive.

During the 1960's a Melbourne psychiatrist, F. Hocking, interviewed some three hundred immigrants to Australia who had undergone extreme stress during World War II. Some had survived the concentration camps or the wartime ghettos. Others had spent long periods hiding out to escape the Nazi dragnets.

As was the case with *mørketiden*, the survivors of the camps recalled that their characteristic apathy and depression began *after* they were liberated.

Furthermore, the effects of camp life appeared to be irreversible. Twenty-five years later the survivors were still visibly withdrawn and depressed. By contrast the fugitives who had hidden out in the woods were still tense and anxious. Both sets of symptoms were so obvious that Dr. Hocking claims to be able to distinguish onetime prisoners from onetime fugitives just by watching them as they sit in his waiting room.

The camp syndrome appears to be the same regardless of whether the institution is a severe one—such as a German concentration camp or a Soviet forced-labor camp—or an ordinary prisoner-of-war camp or even a civil prison. As with combat stress, the symptoms are irritability, hypersensitivity, quickness to take offense, lack of initiative, progressive apathy, and finally complete withdrawal, which may end in death. Among those afflicted with this most extreme form of camp sickness were the *Musselmänner* of the German camps and a distressingly large number of American prisoners in the camps of North Korea.

Wartime stress has produced some less debilitating but

more idiosyncratic symptoms. The Dutch psychiatrist Joost Merloo found that his skin suddenly darkened after a narrow escape from death at Nazi hands. This condition ("fear melanosis") lasted for three years.

The returns are not yet in on the Americans taken prisoner during the Vietnam War. The initial optimism gave way to concern when some of the ex-POW's took their own lives. In the end there is no reason to expect that their experience will be any different from that of other groups of prisoners. All will be marked to some extent.

Those who best survive the extreme stress of prison often appear to be sustained by a strong faith, which can be either religious or secular. In the German camps both the Jehovah's Witnesses and the socialists are remembered for their resistance to the morale-shattering conditions.

Conversely the controversy over the behavior of Americans in the North Korean camps acquired its sharpness from the charge that these young men had succumbed to hopelessness or had made themselves useful to the enemy because they had nothing to believe in.

But even faith is not a perfect shield. Under enough stress anybody will break down.

We would all like to believe that the effects of extreme stress are reversible and that with rest and tender care the victim will return to his former state of health. Unhappily this is not the case.

Like the survivors of concentration camps, war veterans are marked for life, and our veterans' hospitals are still full of former soldiers suffering from the stresses of World War II and the Korean conflict. In Japan people who survived the bombings of Hiroshima and Nagasaki are still reported to be suffering from *bura-bura* sickness, which can mean either the lingering illness or the do-nothing illness. The symptoms are familiar: apathy and withdrawal, nausea, palpitations, and dizziness.

We Americans have been less affected by the horrors of prison camps and warfare than have many other people of the world. Yet, paradoxically, our sufferings from stress seem by any measure to be as severe as those of, say, the Japanese, the English, the Germans, and the Vietnamese, all of whom have endured the terror of massive bombing. In the end the stressors that threaten most of us are not the stressors of extreme situations but the stressors we meet in our everyday lives.

In broad terms we can divide the stressors of everyday life into those that are created by the environment and those that are created by our behavior.

The environmental stresses of modern life are becoming increasingly familiar to us under the impact of the ecology movement. The automobile, considered both as a smog-factory and as a means of transportation, is responsible for stressors that attack both our lungs and our nerves. The discomforts and dangers of big-city life have been much dwelled upon. The stressors of the suburbs strike us at first as milder, but judging by the suburban rates of suicide and alcoholism, life in Greenwich or Evanston or Belvedere can be as stressful as life in Harlem or the South Side of Chicago or Watts.

Urban overcrowding is one of the social stresses that have begun to receive serious attention from the behavioral scientists. Experiments with rats have demonstrated that animals brought up in overcrowded communities are not only ill-natured but tend to be stunted in growth and sexual vigor. Men and rats may not be as far apart as we would like to think.

Noise is a stressor that is almost always with us. For reasons that defy the imagination, the stress of noise has received more attention in Europe than in this country, where our ears are regularly assaulted by the racket produced by high-powered machinery, automobiles, jet airplanes, helicopters, and rock bands.

Laboratory scientists have known for a long time that some strains of mice bred for experimental purposes will go into convulsions and die when they are exposed to a noise that may be as innocuous as the jingling of a ring of keys. A high-pitched air blast is particularly effective, sending the unfortunate animals into uncontrolled dashing about that ends in convulsions and death. These audiogenic seizures, as they are known, are apparently keyed to the animals' circadian rhythms. The highest sensitivity was found to coincide with the highest body temperature.

Human beings are not killed by the effects of high-pitched air blasts, but recent investigations show that noise can produce a variety of serious physiological changes, including interference with the sense of balance, a narrowing of the visual field, changes in color perception, a slowing down of the gastric functions, fatigue, headaches, nausea, constriction of the blood vessels, fluctuations in blood pressure, and even changes in the functioning of the heart. (A sound of about 16,000 cycles per second at about 120 decibels appears to be the most effective.) Virtually the only comforting finding was the lack of any evidence to show that high-level noise interferes with the sexual function.

Many of the most destructive stresses grow out of the demands of our daily work, whether it is parking cars or managing a family or designing office buildings. In industrial jobs the greatest sources of stress include noise, the combined pressure and boredom of doing a repetitive job at a demanding rate of speed, and the human stress of satisfying one's supervisor and co-workers.

As a profession becomes more demanding, the marks of stress become more evident. This proposition was underlined by a recent study of suicide in the medical profession.

A group of investigators led by Dr. Daniel E. DeSole of the Veterans Administration Hospital in Albany, New York, studied the reports of deaths among physicians in three years of the *Journal of the American Medical Association.* They found that about a quarter of deaths among doctors between twenty-five and forty-four years old are suicides. Among the general population of white males of the same age group, the percentage is only 8.5, or one-third as much.

The differences found in suicide rate by specialty were startling:

| Specialty | Rate per 100,000 |
|---|---|
| All physicians | 33 |
| Psychiatrists | 58 |
| Otorhinolaryngologists (ENT) | 46 |
| Anesthesiologists | 44 |
| Ophthalmologists | 39 |
| Urologists | 34 |
| General practitioners | 34 |
| Internists | 31 |
| Pathologists | 30 |
| Obstetricians/gynecologists | 25 |
| Surgeons | 22 |
| Pediatricians | 17 |
| Radiologists | 17 |

A similar study carried out at the Medical College of Pennsylvania, in Philadelphia, revealed the distressing information that women physicians kill themselves at a rate three times higher than women in the general population. Furthermore, physicians are known to suffer from the highest alcoholism rate of any profession. (Alcoholism is, of course, closely related to suicide.) In California each year 450 physicians are forced to give up their practice because of alcoholism, according to Dr. Charles E. Becker of the University of California Medical School.

It is not beyond the powers of a layman to speculate on the staggering rate of suicide among psychiatrists (58!) as compared to pediatricians, with a mere 17. One wonders, however, why anesthesiologists show twice the suicide rate of their operating-room colleagues, the surgeons. Or why the ear-nose-throat men, with a placid specialty that involves comparatively few dramatic emergencies or night calls, should rank second only to the psychiatrists.

DeSole finds the answer in the extraordinary demands

that are made on the doctor to live up to the expectations of the role he plays. The psychiatrist is particularly vulnerable, for he is frequently faced with the opportunity for failure that is built into his imprecise specialty. The surgeon feels comparatively less role strain because success in his specialty depends to a greater extent on simple technical competence.

DeSole concludes, "To a degree unknown to the other professions, the physician is unable to reduce psychological tensions stretched to the emotional breaking point."

The old advice still holds: "Physician, heal thyself!"

# 2
# Stress Diseases

## STRESS AND HYPERTENSION

TWENTY-FIVE million Americans suffer from hypertension, or high blood pressure. This amounts to one-eighth of the entire population, or one out of five American adults. Half the sufferers don't know they are hypertensive.

Each year about 60,000 Americans die of high blood pressure, not counting those in whom hypertension has contributed to death by heart disease or stroke. An even larger number are crippled for normal living.

My friend Mory was a highly driven salesman, a handsome, well-spoken man with a good-looking wife and five bright and attractive children. Mory and his family lived in a San Francisco suburb that is generally considered to be the embodiment of the American middle-class dream.

There was only one trouble. Mory hated selling. I don't mean that he ever told anybody this. Quite the contrary, whenever he mentioned his work to me, he was never anything but enthusiastic. Selling insurance was a great job and he was performing an important service to mankind and things were just going to go on getting better and better. Mory was a salesman, remember, and he had to believe his own message.

The trouble was that selling is a ruthlessly competitive business. Mory was destroyed by the competitiveness. He began to drink more and more, and then, one afternoon after a long lunch, there were angry words at the office and suddenly Mory was without a job.

Mory was pushing forty and jobs weren't easy to find. Much to everybody's surprise, Mory took a job as a landscape gardener. It was a good move. He drank less and he slept through the night instead of tossing while long columns of overdue bills marched through his mind. But he couldn't make enough money landscape-gardening to support his wife and the five children in that desirable suburb; so when a selling job in the city came up, Mory took it.

The cycle repeated itself after a couple of years. This time Mory and his wife had to sell their house and buy a cheaper one. A few months later there was another blowup. A blowup at work was followed by a blowup at home, which ended with Mory packing a bag and moving out. His wife got along as best she could while Mory lived in a rented room and again worked as a gardener. I saw him during this period and thought he looked better than he had for years. His color was good, he was drinking nothing stronger than beer, and he'd quit smoking.

But the unpaid bills finally got to him again, there were threats of foreclosure by the bank, and Mory looked up an old friend who found a job for him. Selling.

He lasted a couple more years before he collapsed on a sidewalk in downtown San Francisco one day. He was dead on arrival at the emergency room, dead of a massive stroke at the age of forty-seven.

Hypertension is not only a killer disease but it is also a disease about which extraordinarily little is known by the medical profession and which cannot be "cured." (There is a medical-school joke that goes like this—Question: What should you do if you discover you have *low* blood pressure? Answer: Fall on your knees and thank God.)

Nobody has a satisfactory explanation of the causes of hypertension. Heredity is thought to have a predisposing effect. The kidneys are regarded with suspicion because they often become involved. Obesity often accompanies the disease. Emotional stress is generally regarded as a major factor.

Hypertension is often first diagnosed in people in their thirties. The life expectancy after diagnosis is about twenty years for those suffering from "essential" hypertension, the more common form of the disease. It is only two years for those suffering from the malignant or accelerated form. Death comes from congestive heart failure, myocardial infarction (a "coronary"), a stroke, or uremia. None of the drugs that have been developed to combat hypertension is entirely satisfactory.

As a stress disease, hypertension is most marked among the black people of our inner-city ghettos, where it is an epidemic affecting as many as a third of the population. This dreadful fact is well known in the black communities and virtually unknown among whites. (I made this discovery myself only a couple of years ago when I was working as a consultant to the Drew postgraduate medical school, a largely black institution in the heart of the Watts-Willowbrook ghetto.)

Why does hypertension strike blacks more often than it strikes whites?

Back in 1949 Franz Alexander, whose great work was to help make psychosomatic medicine respectable, drew attention to the fact that while hypertension was virtually unknown among African blacks, it was extremely common among blacks in America.

Alexander pointed out that the crucial factor appeared to be the blacks' traditional social situation in America. The black has been obliged to accept and endure a lifetime of slights and insults, as well as more substantial outrages against his person and his idea of himself. He has been punished, sometimes by death, when he gives in to the natural response of striking back when injured.

In the words of two eloquent black psychiatrists, William H. Grier and Price M. Cobb, the epidemic of high blood pressure in the ghetto comes from "being black, and perpetually angry, and unable to express it or do anything about it."

The critical factor is the social situation rather than the genetic inheritance of black people. This was demonstrated in 1966 and 1967, when Dr. Ernest Harburg and his associates at the University of Michigan carried out a pilot survey among blacks living in high-stress and low-stress areas of Detroit. The factors considered in grading the relative amounts of stress were socioeconomic level, crime rate, residential change, family breakdown, and overcrowding. Two hundred and eighty people from fifty-six families were interviewed and their blood pressures taken.

In the high-stress area 32 percent of the people examined had high blood pressure. In the low-stress area, only 19 percent were hypertensive. Dr. Harburg cautiously refrained from drawing any final conclusions but the message of his study is clear: Hypertension is a stress disease.

What can we do about the hypertension epidemic?

The strategies of medical treatment can generally be divided into those that are directed toward the individual patient and those that are directed toward the environment. Hypertension is an excellent case in point.

Clearly the greatest good could be done for the greatest number of people by directing our resources toward improving the qualities of the environment that are responsible for the hypertension epidemic. Reducing the tension that is so much a part of American life would have a far more profound effect on the incidence of hypertension than any purely medical strategy. This, however, calls for a social revolution that is not likely to come about.

On the side of individual curative medicine, in spite of a vast amount of research, hypertension remains one of the most frustrating of the major diseases, both for the physician and for the victim. Treatment measures include the control of diet and the use of drugs that have unfortunate side effects. There seems little chance of a breakthrough at this level in either our understanding of hypertension or our ability to control the disease.

It is entirely too early to announce that the brightest hope for the control of hypertension comes from research projects that have developed techniques of letting go, either through Eastern meditative practices or through biofeedback. Yet there is growing evidence that this may be the case.

First, however, let us explore the role of stress in other diseases that cripple and kill.

## STRESS AND THE HEART

All of us who know him kept telling Callahan that he was going to die either of a stroke or a coronary. A bearded, round-bellied Falstaffian man of fifty, Callahan has been living at top speed all his life. Not only does he regularly push himself beyond all reasonable bounds in the course of his work, at which he is remarkably gifted, but he exerts the force of his powerful personality on everyone around him. Those of us who have stayed up all night with Callahan, either working with him or drinking with him or sometimes doing both at the same time, alternately love him and hate him.

I've forgotten now whether the stroke or the coronary came first, and it doesn't particularly matter. The heart attack was the classic myocardial infarction, the painful, cataclysmic, and often fatal seizure that is brought on when the supply of blood to the heart is cut off. Callahan survived, but part of his heart muscle died and there is now scar tissue in its place. Since then he has had a second coronary as well as a stroke that partially paralyzed him for a while.

Callahan is living on a disability pension but continues to work furiously at unpaid jobs. He has taken instruction in a tension-relieving system called progressive relaxation, which was developed by Dr. Edmund Jacobson at his well-known clinic in Chicago. Callahan's attempts to escape from stress have been only partly successful, however, probably because he is by nature a stress-filled person. He simply refuses to slow down, and he knows that his final coronary may come next week, or next month, or next year. When I look at Callahan, I can see the pain in his eyes.

Heart attacks of Callahan's sort strike more than a million

Americans each year. About a third of the victims are less than sixty-five years old. Males outnumber females three to one. A healthy American male runs a one-in-five chance of having a heart attack before he reaches the age of sixty-five.

All this is generally known. What is not generally understood, however, is that sudden death from heart attacks is becoming more and more common among younger people and particularly among women who have assumed positions of responsibility.

A pioneering study carried out by an Army pathologist during the Korean War revealed the vulnerability of even very young and healthy men to heart attacks. The pathologist autopsied soldiers killed in battle to find out how many of them showed the blocking of the coronary arteries that is a prelude to a myocardial infarction. Although the average age of the soldiers was only twenty-two, the investigator discovered that 77 percent had fatty deposits on the walls of their arteries. In 10 percent of the cases the deposits had already occluded over 70 percent of one or more of their major arteries.

Of the 675,000 Americans who died of heart attacks in 1972, more than 175,000, or 26 percent, were younger than sixty-five. The death rate from heart attacks among men between twenty-five and forty-four years old has risen 14 percent during the past twenty years. The rise among older men is not as great.

As for women, there has been an 11 percent rise in deaths from heart disease in women under forty-five years old during the past seven years, according to the National Heart and Lung Institute. Researchers think the increase may be due to a change in life-style, partly involving the new roles that women are taking on in a business world formerly dominated by men. Woman's liberation has its price, and it is a severe one.

It is also significant that people moving from other countries to the United States assume the high rate of coronary heart disease that obtains in this country. Japanese in Japan enjoy one of the lowest rates of coronary heart disease in the world, but Japanese in California suffer heart attacks in precisely the same numbers as other Californians—which is to say, at ten to thirteen times the Japanese rate.

In the midst of all the public concern and medical research directed toward heart disease, the role played by stress has remained unknown. It is generally agreed that the factors that contribute to heart disease include too high a level of fatty substances such as cholesterol in the blood, high blood pressure, high blood sugar, obesity, an improper diet, lack of exercise, and cigarette smoking. A nod is often given in the direction of stress, but its importance as a factor contributing to heart disease is not so widely accepted.

Evidence is beginning to accumulate, however, of a direct relationship between stress and heart disease. Among those contributing to our understanding of this relationship is Dr. Meyer Friedman, a cardiologist whose work at Mount Zion Hospital in San Francisco has attracted much attention.

Dr. Friedman is a maverick in a profession in which the conventional wisdom is to advise potential heart patients (or those recovering from an attack) to watch their diets, lose weight, quit smoking, and to exercise regularly and moderately. The land is full of joggers, each of whom hopes he is warding off a coronary.

"To us, jogging is murder," Dr. Friedman has said, adding that anybody over thirty-five who wants to jog should first have an EEG taken and repeated at regular intervals. He explains that the kind of person who takes up jogging is exactly the type of person who is a prime candidate for a heart attack.

Dr. Friedman has divided the male of the species into two categories, Type A and Type B. The Type A man, he estimates, runs seven times the risk of coronary heart disease as the Type B man. The conviction that these personality types are the key factor in heart attacks is the outcome of almost twenty years of research. Although Dr. Friedman's findings are not by any means generally accepted by cardiologists, his theories are gaining strength and support.

There is a clear reflection of the folk wisdom in Friedman's findings. The Type A man, the candidate for the coronary, is ambitious, aggressive, self-confident, self-demanding, competitive, driven by the clock and by his overwhelming need for success. He is, in fact, the stereotype of the high-pressure businessman who has universally been seen as headed for high blood pressure, a stroke, or a coronary.

Type B is a different person. He may be as serious as the Type A man, but he is easier on himself and more patient with other people, and he doesn't carry his job around with him twenty-four hours a day. Away from the office, Type A may whack a golf ball around the course with the same intensity with which he takes part in an executive committee meeting. Type B may loaf.

Dr. Friedman told Walter McQuade, "A's have no respect for B's, but the smart B uses an A. The great salesmen are A's. The corporation presidents are usually B's."

Dr. Friedman maintains that the Type A syndrome is an unrecognized sickness. He has admitted, a little grimly, that he himself is Type A. (He suffered a heart attack in 1967.)

Most remarkably, Type B's appear to be virtually immune to coronaries. As Dr. Friedman has declared flatly, to the audible distress of other cardiologists, "In the absence of the Type A behavior pattern, coronary heart disease almost never occurs before 70 years of age, regardless of the fatty foods eaten, the cigarettes smoked, or the lack of exercise."

It would be both foolish and ignorant to belittle the importance of these factors. Yet, as research proceeds, both at the Mount Zion institute and elsewhere, it appears likely that the single greatest cause of coronary heart disease is personality and the stress of life.

Evidence tending to corroborate the stress theory of heart

disease recently emerged from a ten-year study of the cardiac health of Seventh Day Adventist men. Seventh Day Adventists are members of a sect that celebrates the Sabbath on Saturday and believes there will be a literal, personal, and visible return of Jesus Christ to this earth. They do not use alcohol, coffee, or tea, and they eat little meat. Both in personality and in style of life, SDA's differ markedly from the run of Americans.

Although heart disease is still the prime killer of male SDA's, the first attack comes ten years later than with non-SDA men, according to Dr. Richard T. Walden of Loma Linda University's medical school, where young men and women prepare for medical missionary work.

Dr. Walden also found that SDA's were relatively free of the symptoms of other diseases in which stress is thought to be a factor, such as rheumatism, cirrhosis of the liver, and lung cancer.

One's life-style can significantly delay the onset of a degenerative disease, Dr. Walden concluded; it cannot hold it off forever.

An entirely different point of view, that of the researcher in public health, adds another dimension to the problem of the coronary heart attack and illuminates the fact, which by now should be plain, that we understand very little indeed about the real origins of heart disease. As Dr. Michael De Bakey, the distinguished cardiac surgeon, has said, "The central issue in heart research is still the fact we don't understand what causes heart disease in the first place."

Noting that the residents of industrial states such as New York, Pennsylvania, New Jersey, and California suffer more often from coronary heart disease than do the residents of rural states such as Iowa, Nebraska, and the Dakotas, Dr. S. Leonard Syme, of the University of California's school of public health, set out to gather evidence on the impact of social stress on heart disease.

Dr. Syme found that social change appears to be an important risk factor and seems to operate quite independently of genetic, dietary or similar factors.

The evidence led Dr. Syme to three conclusions:

First, men whose life situation is different from that in which they grew up run an increased risk of a coronary. A North Dakota farm boy who moves to the big city to take a white-collar job increases his risk three times. If he takes a blue-collar job in the city, however, the risk is increased by only a small amount. Differences in diet, smoking habits, physical activity, obesity, blood pressure and age—all supposed to be critical factors—were found to have no significant bearing on the case.

Secondly, the risk is increased if the man's life situation changes frequently. The more often a man changes his job, the more likely he is to have a coronary.

Thirdly, as a rural area becomes urbanized and industrialized, the risk of heart disease increases also.

Dr. Syme's belief in the relation of social stress to heart disease echoes Alvin Toffler's concept of the generally destructive consequences of "future shock" and the life-change studies at the University of Washington by Dr. Thomas H. Holmes.

Like Holmes, Syme argues that people should not be discouraged from trying to better their lives because to do so invites serious disease. Nor does he believe that we should give up our efforts to control heart disease through better dietary and smoking habits.

"However," he concludes, "these efforts will not significantly alter the magnitude of the nation's problem of heart disease. An environmental approach is needed to achieve this goal, and social stress provides a useful starting point."

Further evidence that stress may be a more important cause of heart attacks than diet or cigarette smoking is at hand in the sad and instructive story of Roseto, Pennsylvania, the so-called Miracle Town where nobody under the age of forty-seven had ever had a heart attack.

Roseto was founded in the 1880's by immigrants from the

town of Roseto in southern Italy. The men found work in the neighboring slate quarries, and the Rosetans went on living as they had in Italy—their lives characterized by a warm community feeling, by close family ties, and by the consumption of vast quantities of food and wine.

As the years went on, Roseto acquired a reputation for its heroic eating habits. Meals would go on for hours while everybody at the table would put away pounds of pasta and dishes rich in olive oil and lard. According to the theories that a high-cholesterol diet brings on heart attacks, the Rosetans were simply committing suicide.

But the curious thing was that in Roseto the death rate, particularly from heart disease, was remarkably low. Dr. John G. Bruhn of the University of Texas medical branch at Galveston visited Roseto in 1961 to look into its growing reputation as a healthy place to live. He found that in spite of the cholesterol-rich diet, the citizens of Roseto suffered heart attacks at a rate one-third the national average and one-fourth the rate of their neighbors in more Americanized towns. They lived to ripe old ages. Dr. Bruhn hypothesized that the warm and close communal and family life in the Italian style was the factor that protected Rosetans from heart attacks.

His hypothesis was sadly borne out when Bruhn returned to Roseto in 1971. "We were stunned," he said.

Bruhn found that during the ten years he had been away, Roseto had turned into a typical American town. The average income had jumped to nearly $12,000. Men were commuting to executive jobs out of town. Children were going away to college. Television had displaced conversation. The cars on the streets were newer and larger. The great American competition of buying and showing off was in full swing. Families no longer sat down at the table for long and leisurely and cholesterol-soaked meals. Now they ate on the run.

And the heart-attack rate had leaped to three times the national average.

"In Roseto, family and community support is disappearing. Most of the men who have had heart attacks here were living under stress and really had nowhere to turn to relieve that pressure," Dr. Bruhn said. "These people have given up something to get something, and it's killing them."

The story of Roseto is a profoundly American and profoundly distressing story.

## STRESS AND CANCER

A man I know (whom I shall call John Knox) was one of the 650,000 Americans in whom cancer was diagnosed in 1973. His case is an interesting one because he is convinced that his cancer was brought on by unusually stressful circumstances that he had to endure for several months.

Employed as an editorial consultant, Knox was obliged during the course of a long and complex piece of work to take on a colleague whom he found to be personally obnoxious. For reasons of company politics, he could not simply ask that his unwanted helper be taken off the job. Instead he swallowed his anger and soldiered on.

The other man was a grand master at all the many games by which human beings manipulate each other. At the end of a day's work with him, Knox would be a basket case. As Knox described the situation to me, "After just a couple of hours with that son of a bitch I feel as if all the energy had been squeezed out of my body. He's going to kill me yet."

He almost did. Knox congratulated himself that he was still alive and reasonably sane when the job was finally finished and his obnoxious helper went back to his own office for good. These congratulations were, Knox now thinks, premature. Two months later he began to be seriously annoyed by a furious itching sensation between his shoulder blades. There was a large mole there, about the size of his little fingernail, which he had had as long as he could remember but which had never troubled him before.

Knox took his problem to his doctor, who excised the mole and told Knox that was probably the end of it. A couple of days later, however, Knox's phone rang and he learned that the lab had reported that the mole was malignant. He went into the hospital, this time to have several square inches of skin peeled off his back as a precautionary measure.

That was a year ago. Knox's cancer has not recurred. His doctor is keeping a sharp eye on him, particularly on his lymph glands, and will continue to do so for the next four years. Knox is convinced that the three months of acute psychological stress he endured was the trigger that turned the mole on his back into a melanoma. He has taken up meditation and tells me that absolutely nothing would induce him to put up again with the stressful situation he thinks came so close to killing him.

The relation of stress to cancer is even less widely accepted than is the relation of stress to heart disease and high blood pressure. There is important evidence, however, that stress may indeed be a key factor in the origins of this still mysterious disease.

In a study completed in 1955 Lawrence Le Shan and Richard E. Worthington of the Institute of Applied Biology discovered that three principal psychological characteristics were more common among cancer patients than among people not suffering from cancer.

The great majority of the cancer patients had suffered the loss of an important personal relationship before their disease was diagnosed—and presumably before their disease began.

Just under half the patients showed an apparent inability to express hostile feelings toward other people.

More than a third of the cancer patients showed tension over the death of one of their parents, an event that had often occurred far in the past.

So far as I know, in the twenty years since these findings were reported, they have not been followed up.* Their im-

* As this book went to press, I became aware of the work of Dr. Rene Mastrovito of the Memorial Sloan-Kettering Cancer Center who told a recent cancer conference about patients who have developed cancer after psychological trauma, usually the loss of a loved one or a job.

portance indicates they certainly should be, for if social stress is indeed an important factor, we should redirect the thrust of our current and highly publicized "war" against cancer, which is geared largely to testing magic bullets.

Support for the social-stress theory of cancer has come recently from Loma Linda University's medical school, where it has been found that, as in the case of heart attacks, Seventh Day Adventists succumb to cancer at a much lower rate than do the rest of us. The ratio is about one to three, which is a powerful argument in favor of the sense of acceptance and serenity that apparently follows from membership in that sect.

A curious sidelight on the relation of stress to cancer has been reported by a Greek researcher, Dr. H. C. Rassidakis, who has discovered that in Greece, England, Wales, Scotland, and the USSR, the mentally ill die from cancer at only about one-third the rate of the general population. Schizophrenics are the most resistant, perhaps because they have the least contact with reality.

Animal experiments have buttressed the importance of social stress in cancer. In many laboratories changing the conditions of stress have resulted in changes in the onset and progress of cancers in animals.

An example of this work was reported in the spring of 1972 from the Virginia Polytechnic Institute. Dr. W. B. Gross, a professor of veterinary medicine, found that mental stress had a remarkable effect on the production of cancer among chickens.

The cancer Dr. Gross worked with was a virus-induced tumor called Marek's Disease. Two flocks of chickens were exposed to birds suffering from Marek's Disease, but in two significantly different environments.

The first flock lived as chickens normally do, with their social life being governed by a clearly recognized pecking order. Only 3 percent of these birds developed the cancer.

The experimenters interfered with the pecking order in the other flock of birds, raising up the lowly and humbling the mighty, and thus producing a high-stress environment. Twenty-three percent of these birds succumbed—or almost eight times as many as among the low-stressed birds.

Within the past ten years the theory that cancer is caused by a virus has acquired scientific respectability. Since the mid-1960's investigators have been particularly interested in the herpes viruses, a family that is better known for its association with cold sores and fever blisters.

Recent investigators, including Dr. Albert Sabin of polio-vaccine fame, have reported an association between the herpes simplex viruses (HSV) and a variety of cancers, including cancer of the uterus, the mouth, the bladder, the prostate, the kidney, and the lymphatic system.

This promising work is at the stage at which it contains more puzzles than answers. It is far too early to jump to any conclusions. Yet there is a possibility that the HSV's are the key to the relation between stress and cancer. We know that stress is a prime factor in producing other, though minor, HSV-related conditions, such as cold sores. Stress may turn out to be the trigger mechanism in bringing about HSV-related cancers also.

The problem is further illuminated by considering the incidence of cancer among groups of people who are under unusual stress. Dr. Jack E. White, who directs the cancer research center at Howard University medical school, has recently reported the alarming fact that from 1950 to 1967 mortality rates for all types of cancer among black males jumped 50 percent. For both sexes, the increase in mortality from cancer was 20 percent. During these years there was no comparable increase among whites of either sex.

The death rates are even more remarkable and distressing for specific types of cancer. American blacks now appear to have the world's highest mortality rates from cancer of the pancreas and cancer of the prostate, and are heading toward the highest rate in cancer of the esophagus.

Are these cancers related to stress?

Dr. White tends to attribute the increase of cancer among

blacks to environmental factors, such as increased exposure to pollutants in the air when the blacks move from the farm into cities, but he does not ignore the stress factor. Whether the critical points of adaptability to a new environment can be found in physical processes (for instance, exposure to pollutants) or in emotional processes is a question that demands an answer.

If evidence that a high-stress environment is favorable to cancer continues to accumulate, we must surely revise our thinking about the origins and control of cancer. A magic bullet may yet be found, but again it may not. Until it is, it would be foolish, wasteful, and inhumane to refrain from mounting a major research effort directed toward the relationship between stress and cancer.

## STRESS AND SEX

Over his fifth scotch on the rocks, my friend Turner sighed and said he hadn't expected to find himself over the hill at the age of forty-six. I sweetened his drink and asked him what his trouble was. "Oh, Christ," he said glumly, "I just can't get it up anymore. Jeanie and I used to make it three or four times a week. Now I'm lucky if I can do it once a month. Do you remember that scene in the movie *Hospital* in which George C. Scott delivers an oration about his limp dingus? Well, that's your old friend Turner, too."

As he went on talking it became clear that this wasn't the only thing troubling him. He was being pushed hard at the office by a young man who wanted his job, his oldest daughter had at the age of sixteen moved out of the house and into a commune of Jesus freaks, and as Turner's sexual performance decreased, his other relations with his wife had too.

As was the case with George C. Scott in the movie, things worked out for Turner. On a long assignment in a city far from the stress of home and office, Turner found himself in bed with a pleasant, attractive, and undemanding woman.

He'd had just enough to drink to relieve his fears that he was going to fail again.

"Four times," he told me. *"Four times.* How's that for an old man?"

Unhappily the sexual problems caused by stress are not all relieved as pleasantly as were Turner's.

In men impotence and premature ejaculation are notoriously the effects of stress. Furthermore, stress not only inhibits the sexual urge but also diminishes the formation of sperm cells. In women frigidity is a common consequence of life stress. Stress causes menstruation to become irregular and (to the terror of wayward adolescent girls) can cause the menses to stop entirely. Nursing mothers find that their yield of milk falls off when they are under stress.

The sexual performance of a man is linked to his production of a powerful hormone called testosterone. Recent research by Dr. Robert Rose and his colleagues at the Boston University School of Medicine has demonstrated that there is a seesaw relationship between stress and testosterone. As stress goes up, testosterone goes down.

The first part of the study was carried out by measuring the testosterone levels in the urine of soldiers in Vietnam awaiting an enemy attack, of infantrymen in training, and of Army men in nonstressful situations.

The testosterone levels of the men under stress proved to be remarkably lower than the levels of the unstressed men—about as low as you can get in a normal male—proving once again that when a man is seriously worried about survival he has little interest in making love.

Dr. Rose verified these results with studies of students in Officers' Candidate School. During the first weeks, when the candidates were in danger of being flunked from the course, their testosterone levels fell; after they had passed the danger point and were reasonably sure of surviving, both their testosterone levels and their interest in females rose dramatically.

New light on the relationship of stress and sex—and particularly the relationship between stress and homosexuality—has been provided by the recent work of Dr. Ingeborg Ward of Villanova University. Dr. Ward's work has shown that if a pregnant rat experiences severe stress, her male offspring will be born with different behavior patterns from normal male rat pups, showing low levels of masculine behavior and even engaging in typically female behavior (such as allowing themselves to be mounted by aggressive males).

Dr. Ward's pregnant rats were stressed by being cooped up in Plexiglas tubes, which were then placed under strong, glaring lights. The stress produced in this way was so great that some of the animals died. Others showed typical stress-induced physical reactions that are not much different from human reactions. They urinated and defecated and their hair stood on end. When their pups were born, some were exposed to further stress by being shaken on vibrating metal racks.

After they had grown to puberty, which for a rat takes about 90 days, the pups from stressed mothers showed significantly different patterns of sexual behavior from the control, or normal, pups. When placed in the company of a female rat in heat, the pups from the stressed litters copulated far less often than the normal pups.

Dr. Ward continued her investigation by castrating the pups from both stressed and unstressed litters and then injecting them with the female hormone progesterone. When exposed to vigorous young male rats, the prenatally stressed pups assumed the female role and the female sexual posture.

This behavior, Dr. Ward believes, is brought about by the effect of stress on the development of the fetus during a critical period. Stress causes the pituitary gland to stimulate the production of the adrenal stress hormones. As a result the powerful testosterone is replaced by a weaker male hormone, androsterone.

"The net result," Dr. Ward reported, "was that the testosterone was unable to do its normal job of programming the brain. The tissues developed under the influence of the weaker hormone, and thus the animals were unable to differentiate as normally functioning males."

There is a clear suggestion here that human homosexuality may turn out to be the result of prenatal stress in the mother—a hypothesis which, if it can be established, will have farreaching social and moral consequences.

Among the broader implications is the suggestion that the production of homosexuals is nature's way of limiting the growth of a population that is living in an overly stressed environment. And if homosexuality is, indeed, the result of faulty prenatal imprinting, we are presented with a thoroughly discouraging answer to the ancient question of whether or not a homosexual's interest can be redirected to the other sex.

The determination of an unborn child's sex has been a matter of consuming interest since the earliest recorded times. Kingdoms and empires have trembled on the question of whether an infant is to be a boy or a girl. Recently Dr. Donald Schuster and his wife, Dr. Locky Schuster, both psychologists at Iowa State, have discovered that a child's sex may be determined by the relative stress at the time of conception.

If the mother is mildly stressed whenever she makes love but the father is unstressed, the Schusters report that their children will tend to be boys. If the father is stressed but his wife isn't, most of their children will be girls. If neither is under stress, their children will be of both sexes. If they are both severely stressed, they may have no children at all.

## STRESS AND AGING

Judging from the evidence at hand, it seems likely that whenever we sigh and complain that a particularly harrowing experience has taken ten years off our life, we are speaking the truth.

The relation between stress and aging (unlike the relationship between stress and cancer) is one we are prepared to accept without controversy. It is simply a matter of common observation that, with some notable exceptions, people who live hard lives tend to wear out earlier.

A most striking illustration of the relationship of life stress and physical age was offered to me when, in the course of writing a magazine article, I became involved with a group of ex-priests and ex-nuns. Although the priests' apparent age matched their real age, the nuns, women for the most part between thirty and forty, all looked five to ten years younger than their real ages—their skin was clearer and less wrinkled, their eyes were brighter, their faces less mature.

My nonscientific observations of the general resistance of nuns to killing diseases and particularly to cancer received support when I became aware of the work of Dr. Con Fecher of Dayton, Ohio, a statistician who has been studying the health of nuns since 1925. Dr. Fecher has reported that nuns under the age of sixty experience less than one-half the deaths from all causes than do women generally. Cancer of the cervix is extraordinarily rare, while the rates of death from other common cancers—stomach, liver, gallbladder, pancreas, and rectum—are half the rate for the general population.

When I commented on the youthfulness of the ex-nuns, one of the ex-priests (who was himself married to an ex-nun) laughed and remarked that it was not an unusual comment. Although the modern nun is rarely sequestered in a convent, she is relieved of the stresses of finding and holding a job, of managing a sex life, or of living with obstreperous relatives—although an obstreperous mother superior is probably a worthy substitute. The circumstances of convent life usually impose less wear and tear, and this relative tranquility slows down the aging process.

The other side of this argument, of course, is that the nuns who leave the convent take upon themselves a full measure of stress. There is a ready-made field for investigation in comparing the medical histories of ex-nuns with those of their sisters who remain in the convents.

The violent times in which we live have produced more than enough stress to give us examples of premature aging brought on by stress processes. A most strikingly stressed population is made up of the survivors of the bombings of Hiroshima and Nagasaki, events which because of their uniqueness produced emotional stress more severe than anything produced on a mass scale in the European war—even the concentration camps.

Robert Jay Lifton's widely admired study of the psychological warping of the survivors has described this aspect of their experience to a wide audience. Less well-known studies have shown that these unfortunate people suffer from patterns of illness and death typical of people fifteen to twenty years older than they are.

On a less dramatic but broader level, it has been suggested that the increasingly common phenomenon of jet lag may be a form of aging due to stress. Jet lag is a period of lowered effectiveness caused by the shift in time as we travel around the world at high speed. Body-time falls out of phase with environment-time. It is not an agreeable experience.

In its most extreme form, as described by veteran airline pilots, jet lag is made up of headaches, trouble with focusing the eyes, gastrointestinal upsets and loss of appetite, shortness of breath, sweating, and nightmares.

A doctor once told the Flying Physicians Association that he had observed symptoms of premature aging particularly in pilots flying east-west runs. (One might hope they would regain their lost youth on the west-east runs. This is a frivolous observation, but it points up the important fact that the ravages of stress are irreversible. We can never recover lost ground by retracing our steps.)

The irreversibility of the aging process is a matter of utmost importance. Hans Selye, the Austrian-Canadian physician who is the leading living authority on stress, has proposed that each of us inherits a fixed store of vitality with which to meet the stress of life. We can hoard this vitality or we can spend it lavishly in the course of a stressful life. As our vitality (which Selye also calls adaptational energy) is used up, we grow older and suffer from the physical symptoms of aging. When this energy has been entirely used up, we die.

Selye has put the matter memorably: "Vitality is like a special kind of bank account which you can use up by withdrawal but cannot increase by deposits. Your only control over this most precious fortune is the rate at which you make your withdrawals. The solution is evidently not to stop withdrawing, for this would be death. Nor is it to withdraw just enough for survival, for this would permit only a vegetative life, worse than death. The intelligent thing to do :s to withdraw generously, but never expend wastefully."

As was the case with hypertension, heart disease, and cancer, we can see the usefulness of mounting parallel and complementary—rather than antagonistic—assaults on the aging process. The first attack would continue the search for drugs that are useful in managing particular degenerative diseases, and possibly in slowing down the general aging process. The second would seriously investigate the possibilities of prolonging life by changing both the general and the individual environment.

As we proceed with this book, we will direct our attention to methods by which each of us can withdraw vitality generously without expending it wastefully.

## STRESS AND ULCERS

A peptic ulcer is a hole that has been eaten into the lining of the stomach or duodenum (the first portion of the small intestine) by the acid juices that aid the process of digestion.

Since all our stomachs contain these acids, a real and unexplained puzzle is found in the fortunate fact that most of us don't develop ulcers. Another puzzle is the suddenness with which ulcers can strike.

When Cornelius woke up one morning, he knew he had an

ulcer. He'd been worrying about getting an ulcer for a long time and he was familiar with the symptoms: a severe pain in his stomach, heartburn, a feeling that his stomach was swelling up, nausea.

The doctor he went to put Cornelius to bed for a couple of weeks and told him to stop worrying. He prescribed phenobarbital to keep Cornelius calm, and a diet of bland and tasteless foods, with much milk to rest his stomach. The doctor also prescribed an antacid mixture of aluminum hydroxide and magnesium trisilicate, which Cornelius drank in a half-glass of water every couple of hours. The antacid constipated him, for which the doctor prescribed mineral oil.

After a couple of weeks in bed and another couple of weeks taking things easy, Cornelius discovered gratefully that his symptoms were gone. His doctor congratulated him and suggested that he try to arrange his life so that he would be exposed to less stress in the future.

Cornelius finds this a little difficult to do. He and his estranged wife are squabbling over the size of his alimony payments. His landlord is trying to raise the rent of his apartment. The lady he has been keeping company with shows signs of wanting to get married. The law firm of which he is a partner didn't do so well last year. Cornelius keeps a large bottle of the antacid mixture in a drawer of his desk and drinks a generous slug of it whenever he feels twinges from his stomach, which is quite often.

Once I attempted to commiserate with Cornelius about his affliction.

"Oh, hell," he said, "don't you know that only successful men get ulcers?"

He laughed, but he didn't sound as if he thought he'd been very funny.

About five out of every hundred Americans suffer from an ulcer at one time or another. Ten thousand Americans die each year of a peptic ulcer, usually from massive hemorrhage or perforation into the abdominal cavity.

Some researchers have blamed diet for ulcers, but as Dr. I. Mendeloff of Johns Hopkins said recently, "One way to put it is that it's what's eating you rather than what you're eating." Dr. Mendeloff speaks with authority, for he is president of the American Gastroenterological Association.

Ulcers can be the consequence of both psychological and physical stress. Recognition of the part played by physical stress goes back to the Roman physician Celsus, who described the stress ulcers produced in soldiers during rigorous campaigns. Nearly two millenia later, in the mid-1800's, Thomas Blizard Curling, a noted British physician, described the appearance of acute bleeding peptic ulcers in patients suffering from severe burns. (These became known as "Curling's ulcers.")

Some twenty years after Curling's discovery, the great Viennese doctor, Theodor Billroth, the father of modern abdominal surgery, found similar ulcers in patients who had undergone major surgery. In World War II, English doctors were presented with "air-raid" ulcers, which appeared overnight after particularly intense bombing raids.

It is not easy to sort out the role played by physical stress from the role played by psychological stress in any of these cases. Both probably play a part, for similar ulcers can be produced in laboratory animals both by stress that is largely physical and by stress that is largely psychological.

The idea of the "ulcer type" as an ambitious, hard-driving go-getter continues to be lodged firmly in both the popular and the professional mind. It is almost as if a peptic ulcer were a badge of masculinity as it is viewed in the American ethos. Forty years ago the conventional wisdom was that the ulcer was the price paid by a man dominated by ambition and always pressing onward to overcome the obstacles in his way. In buttressing this argument, it was observed that such unambitious types as Chinese coolies and Latin American Indians were spared the suffering of ulcers.

More recent thinking sees the ulcer as a mark of dependency rather than of fierce ambition. As Franz Alexander described the genesis of the ulcer, it gives its victim the opportunity to withdraw from his (or her) responsibilities and to opt out of the race.

The idea of an ulcer as sort of a red badge of courage is simply nonsense. It is rather, as are so many other psychogenic diseases, a costly device to allow the sufferer to adapt to an intolerably stressful situation.

It was not until the early 1970's that investigators at Rockefeller University in New York produced stress ulcers in laboratory mice under conditions that clearly distinguished between psychological stress and physical stress. These experiments led to a theory of ulcer formation that has important human implications.

The essence of the experiment carried out by Dr. Jay M. Weiss and his associates was to subject three rats simultaneously to identical physical stressors but to vary the psychological stress, which involved the predictability of an electric shock delivered to the rats' tails.

A *beep-beep* signal told one rat when to expect a shock. The second rat heard only random *beeps* but felt exactly the same shocks. The third rat was confined in the same uncomfortable position as the other two and had an electrode fastened to his tail, but was not given any shocks at all.

After the three rats had been subjected to their varying degrees of psychological stress, they were sacrificed, opened up, and examined for stomach ulcers, which were then measured.

The results were striking. The control rat, who heard no *beeps* and felt no shocks, developed hardly any ulcers at all. The rat who heard only random *beeps* that had no connection with the shocks he felt, developed ulcers five times larger than the ulcers that developed in his partner, who heard warning *beeps*. Thus, the rat who suffered most of all was the unfortunate one who had to endure helplessly unpredictable stress—the unpredictability being the key factor. The same proposition is probably true for human beings.

## RESPONSES TO STRESS

The same stressor can produce a variety of reactions, each person responding to stress in a manner that is probably determined both by his genetic heritage and by his experience of life. Some people respond by developing an ulcer or high blood pressure, or succumb to a heart attack or cancer. Others break out in eczema or suffer from headaches, back pain, rheumatism, asthma, diarrhea, insomnia, or an entire catalogue of other disabling psychogenic illnesses.

The individuality of response was one of the messages that came out of an extraordinarily interesting series of experiments with rhesus monkeys carried out by Dr. Charles F. Stroebel at the Institute of Living in Hartford, Connecticut. Dr. Stroebel's main interest was in casting light on the influence of stress on the circadian rhythm. In the process he also produced a wide variety of somatic and behavioral responses in the individual monkeys by identical stressors.

Each of the experimental monkeys had implanted in its brain eighteen electrodes leading to electroencephalographs (or EEG's—instruments that measure the electrical activity of the brain). The monkeys were also equipped with electrodes in their muscles, catheters in their hearts, and temperature sensors on their skin.

Each monkey was then placed in an isolation booth, with controlled temperature and humidity. It could reach two levers, one on its right and one on its left. The right-hand lever was used for solving problems devised by the experimenters. The left-hand lever, the monkey soon discovered, could be used to ward off a variety of unpleasant experiences, such as high temperatures, flashing lights, and electric shocks. The monkey quickly learned to keep its hands on the left-hand lever and to pump it constantly just in case something unpleasant was on its way. (The situation was not so far from some human situations as it at first appears.)

The monkeys lived like this for several hours a day for two weeks to a month. Then the researchers retracted the left-hand lever into the wall, where the monkey could see it but couldn't reach it. At the same time the harassments were ended—no more shocks, no more flashing lights, no more unpleasant heat.

Now, a phenomenon occurred that has disturbing parallels in human behavior. Although the monkeys were no longer annoyed by noxious and disturbing stressors, they almost literally went out of their minds trying to get at the magic left-hand lever.

When they failed, all but one of the thirteen animals began to develop neurotic and psychosomatic symptoms. Two began to breathe asthmatically. Another two developed duodenal ulcers that later killed them. Five monkeys suffered from gastrointestinal disturbances and sores that wouldn't heal.

Seven other monkeys displayed neurotic rather than physical symptoms. They were apathetic and gave up grooming themselves. Their appetites fell off. Two of them spent their times catching imaginary flies. One of them masturbated like a simian Portnoy. Three pulled out their own fur.

When two monkeys of each group—psychosomatic and neurotic—were again allowed to operate the left-hand levers, there was a dramatic recovery among the psychosomatic monkeys. The neurotic animals, however, continued their bizarre behavior.

Dr. Stroebel believes that the genetic inheritance of each animal determined the way in which it responded. Those predisposed toward bodily illness became asthmatic or developed ulcers or sores. Those predisposed toward psychoneurotic illness caught flies or masturbated.

There is every reason to believe that what was true of Dr. Stroebel's monkeys is true of animal life in general. And that, of course, includes human beings.

## TESTING FOR STRESS

In Part II we will investigate techniques of letting go and escaping from stress. Before we go on, each of us should measure his susceptibility to the stress diseases. At the University of Washington Medical School in Seattle, Drs. Thomas H. Holmes and Richard H. Rahe devised a test for precisely this purpose.

The work that eventually led to the "Social Readjustment

Rating Scale" began in 1949 when Holmes, the senior of the two, became interested in the life circumstances of tuberculosis patients. By the time the study was finished in 1964 the investigators had concluded that in a remarkable number of cases the onset of the disease had followed serious changes in the lives of the victims—divorce, a death in the family, a move from one place to another, job change.

In 1965 Holmes and Rahe drew up their Social Readjustment Rating Scale as a predictor of general disease or disability—and not just of tuberculosis.

The Holmes-Rahe scale lists forty-three common life changes in the order in which they have been found to be precursors of illness. Some of the changes are disagreeable (such as being fired from one's job) while some are generally considered to be agreeable (such as the Christmas season).

Stress is often a paradox and even outstanding personal achievement appears to contribute to the development of disease. (For instance, early in 1972 Astronaut Edwin "Buzz" Aldrin, Jr., the second man to step on the moon, revealed that he had committed himself to a psychiatric hospital after his "outstanding personal achievement." Explaining what had happened, Aldrin said, "I don't think any of us knew how to handle it.")

The relationship between life change and disease seems to have little to do with culture. The Holmes-Rahe scale has been verified among civilians and Navy men in the United States and in Japan, El Salvador, Spain, Belgium, Sweden, Denmark, and Finland. Its validity was found unchanged wherever it was used.

To find one's own score, simply pencil in the values of the items in the following list that apply to you during the past year. Add up your score and compare it with the range of scores that are given below the test.

If your total score is less than 150, you have only a 37 percent chance of illness during the next two years.

If your score is between 150 and 300, you have a 51 percent chance of becoming sick.

| Rank | Event | Value | Your Score |
|------|-------|-------|------------|
| 1 | Death of spouse | 100 | _____ |
| 2 | Divorce | 73 | _____ |
| 3 | Marital separation | 65 | _____ |
| 4 | Jail term | 63 | _____ |
| 5 | Death of close family member | 63 | _____ |
| 6 | Personal injury or illness | 53 | _____ |
| 7 | Marriage | 50 | _____ |
| 8 | Fired from work | 47 | _____ |
| 9 | Marital reconciliation | 45 | _____ |
| 10 | Retirement | 45 | _____ |
| 11 | Change in family member's health | 44 | _____ |
| 12 | Pregnancy | 40 | _____ |
| 13 | Sex difficulties | 39 | _____ |
| 14 | Addition to family | 39 | _____ |
| 15 | Business readjustment | 39 | _____ |
| 16 | Change in financial status | 38 | _____ |
| 17 | Death of close friend | 37 | _____ |
| 18 | Change to different line of work | 36 | _____ |
| 19 | Change in number of marital arguments | 35 | _____ |
| 20 | Mortgage or loan over $10,000 | 31 | _____ |
| 21 | Foreclosure of mortgage or loan | 30 | _____ |
| 22 | Change in work responsibilities | 29 | _____ |
| 23 | Son or daughter leaving home | 29 | _____ |
| 24 | Trouble with in-laws | 29 | _____ |
| 25 | Outstanding personal achievement | 28 | _____ |
| 26 | Spouse begins or stops work | 26 | _____ |
| 27 | Starting or finishing school | 26 | _____ |
| 28 | Change in living conditions | 25 | _____ |
| 29 | Revision of personal habits | 24 | _____ |
| 30 | Trouble with boss | 23 | _____ |
| 31 | Change in work hours, conditions | 20 | _____ |
| 32 | Change in residence | 20 | _____ |
| 33 | Change in schools | 20 | _____ |
| 34 | Change in recreational habits | 19 | _____ |
| 35 | Change in church activities | 19 | _____ |

| Rank | Event | Value | Your Score |
|------|-------|-------|------------|
| 36 | Change in social activities | 18 | _____ |
| 37 | Mortgage or loan under $10,000 | 17 | _____ |
| 38 | Change in sleeping habits | 16 | _____ |
| 39 | Change in number of family gatherings | 15 | _____ |
| 40 | Change in eating habits | 15 | _____ |
| 41 | Vacation | 13 | _____ |
| 42 | Christmas season | 12 | _____ |
| 43 | Minor violation of the law | 11 | _____ |
| Total | | | _____ |

If your score is more than 300, you are in real danger, for the odds are 80 percent that you will become sick.

And this is not all. As Dr. Holmes, who has a mordant sense of humor, has put it, "If you have more than three hundred life-change units and get sick, the probability is you will have cancer, a heart attack or manic depressive psychosis rather than warts or menstrual irregularities."

But he adds, "There are worse things in this life than illness. It is worse to go on in an intolerable, dull, or demeaning situation."

We are all caught in a great contradiction—perhaps the central contradiction of the human dilemma. Life is growth. Growth is change. Development is change. But change is also a mortal threat, and living is in itself a dangerous business. We have no choice but to accept this threat as the price of living at all, and each of us thereupon becomes his own existential antihero, a character out of Hemingway or Camus.

Even though there is no way to resolve this essential contradiction, we are not entirely helpless. There *are* ways in which each of us, acting on his own behalf, can temper the harshness of the dilemma, can alter the odds in his own favor.

# Part II
## ESCAPE FROM STRESS

# 3
# Letting Go with Meditation

## SCIENTISTS AND MYSTICS

THE FIGHT-OR-FLIGHT syndrome, which was necessary for the survival of primitive man, is today a biological anachronism that often acts to overload our systems with stress. Stress drains our vital reserves of energy, and as we have seen, it is becoming increasingly apparent that this process is associated with the onset of some major diseases—perhaps of all major diseases. Clearly we can help to assure our survival in good health if we can find ways to control our built-in physiological responses to stress.

The general belief has been that many of our body's responses, like the fight-or-flight syndrome, are automatic and beyond control. Recently, however, serious work by reputable scientists is making it increasingly clear that we can learn to exert control over the operations of the autonomic nervous system, which manages such "involuntary" affairs as heart rate, blood pressure, and the secretion of the stress hormones.

We will follow two paths of exploration. One is that of hard science. The other is the path of yoga, Zen, and hypnosis.

Most of us bring with us a prejudice against the second path. Mystics and mysticism, in our eyes, are uncomfortably linked to the ineffable, the religious, and the impractical.

This need not be so. In his novel *Island* the late Aldous Huxley invented the phrase "experimental mysticism" to describe a utopian society that combined Eastern mysticism with Western science. Following Huxley's lead, Joseph T. Hart, an investigator into methods of voluntary control, has more recently coined "pragmatic mysticism" to describe the current scientific interest in mystical practices that have been demonstrated to have practical consequences.

We may be amused or repelled by the cult of the Maharishi Mahesh Yogi that pervades the popular practice of trancendental meditation, but we cannot deny the reports from Harvard Medical School and the University of California at Los Angeles that TM (as transcendental meditation is known) has desirable practical consequences.

We may find autogenic training to be a somewhat gothic, Germanic structure that combines autohypnosis with a mystical component, but we cannot deny the reports of measurable physiological effects that have come from the Menninger Foundation.

We may even come to believe, with Theodore X. Barber of the Medfield Foundation, that there is no such thing as hypnosis, and at the same time we are, like Barber, obliged to admit that hypnosis works.

Our other line of exploration is in a direction more acceptable to the hard-nosed scientists—the biofeedback of muscular responses, of visceral responses, and of neurologic responses. Biofeedback produces many of the same results as pragmatic mysticism, but it does so through the use of delicate electronic devices and the application of new theories of learning.

Since their results are similar, it should not surprise us to find a common thread in meditation, hypnosis, autogenic training, and biofeedback. The common thread is found in the reports of experimental subjects who have done their best to describe what has gone on inside.

When Dr. Joe Kamiya of the Langley-Porter Neuropsychiatric Institute, a pioneer in the biofeedback of brain waves, asked his first subject to try to describe how he produced trains of alpha waves, the man replied that all he was conscious of was "not thinking."

The instructions given me when I was initiated into TM were, "Don't let the thoughts bother you. Just go back to your mantra and the thoughts will go away."

Barber described to me the process of relaxing through autohypnosis: "Imagine that you're floating on a cloud, you're sinking into a soft, cushiony cloud. You're feeling more and more sleepy, it's soft and cottony, you're more and more relaxed."

One of the most expressive reports came from a hypertensive young woman whom Dr. Neal Miller of the Rockefeller University taught to control her blood pressure through biofeedback. "At first it seemed that lowering my pressure was only a simple muscular trick," she wrote. "I thought it was a matter of relaxing my stomach, my chest, my breathing, but none of these worked all the time. I found I could drop my pressure quickly by fooling with my muscles, but I could only sustain the drop if I 'relaxed' my mind. It all seemed to depend on clearing my mind of all stressful thoughts. It's almost the yoga thing, almost self-hypnosis. Usually, when I'm on the cot [in the laboratory] I try to think of my brain as a lake inside my head."

The common thread is now clear, and like all really important discoveries it turns out to be an extraordinarily simple idea. The key to survival is the ability to let go.

The mystic may describe letting go as "cosmic consciousness," but for us it is more useful to think of it as "passive volition," a well-chosen phrase of Dr. Elmer Green of the Menninger Foundation. Letting go is passive, but it is not mere passivity, it is a passive state that paradoxically allows some desired thing to happen.

The scriptural dictum goes, "For whosoever hath, to him shall be given, and he shall have more abundance; but whosoever hath not, from him shall be taken away even that he hath." This is precisely the case with letting go.

Some people are born with a neurophysiological makeup that permits them to let go at will. Others inherit or grow into a nervous system so highly tuned they twang like harps whenever they are touched.

For these unfortunates letting go is almost impossible without expert guidance. The more they try to let go, the harder they hang on. The more they try to relax, the tenser their muscles become. The more they try to make something happen, the more impossible it becomes. And yet they too can learn to let go.

Letting go slows the heart rate. Letting go lowers the blood pressure. Letting go eliminates the headache. Letting go warms the cold hand and dries the sweaty palm.

Practiced regularly, letting go encourages both a habitual emotional calmness and a habitual equilibrium of the physiology. Letting go encourages the parasympathetic nervous system, which acts to calm the bodily functions, and inhibits the sympathetic system, which transmits the signals that set off the fight-or-flight reaction. Letting go encourages the process of homeostasis and enlists the wisdom of the body in the cause of health.

## ALTERED STATES OF CONSCIOUSNESS

During the past decade an increasing body of scientific evidence has pointed in a new direction in the management of stress. The new message is that in order to relieve stress effectively we must make a quantum jump and, without using drugs, enter into states of consciousness that are different in quality from the states of consciousness of our ordinary life.

This message is related to the passionate interest shown since the early 1960's, mainly by young people but also by their elders, in nonordinary, or psychedelic, experience. Their interest has shown itself both in an enthusiastic and uncritical use of drugs and in the adoption of different styles of living and in mystical practices, mainly from the Far East.

Most of this activity is unrelated to stress, but there are many points of tangency between the problems raised by psychedelic experiences and the problems raised by the study of stress.

At universities, medical schools, and other research institutions investigators have in the past few years begun to look into the relationship of nonordinary inner experiences and stress. The gist of their work is that the various ways of letting go—Zen, yoga, transcendental meditation, hypnosis, biofeedback—have measurable and beneficial effects on such stress conditions as high blood pressure, rapid or irregular heartbeat, migraine and tension headaches, and sweaty palms. Whether this general lowering of stress also acts to forestall heart attacks, cancer, or ulcers remains to be proved.

These nonordinary inner experiences are often described as altered states of consciousness, a phrase that describes both the yogi's trance and the experience of the youngster who drops acid, both the "alpha state" produced with the help of an electronic feedback device and the ecstasy of the Christian mystic.

Most of us easily recognize only two states of consciousness—the waking state and the sleeping state. If we are pushed further, we will admit that our sleep does not remain unchanged in texture and quality during the night. There is a clear difference between dreaming sleep and dreamless sleep. (There are in fact four stages of sleep, through which we oscillate in a cycle that takes about ninety minutes.)

Upon reflection, we can recognize that our waking consciousness is not all of the same quality either. There are moments of tense alertness experienced by, for example, a batter waiting for the pitch or a man on trial awaiting the verdict of a jury or a motorist at an unfamiliar and complex highway intersection.

There are occasions when time seems to rush like a river in flood and there are other occasions when it creeps like a glacier. Our "usual" waking state represents only a sort of statistical mean in a daily experience that has an extraordinary variety.

Interspersed in our usual waking state are not only episodes of increased alertness but also interludes we usually describe as daydreaming or reverie. William James, among the greatest of American psychologists, described the daydreaming state with his usual accuracy and grace: "The eyes are fixed on vacancy, the sounds of the world melt into confused unity, the attention is dispersed so that the whole body is felt, as it were, at once, and the foreground of consciousness is filled, if by anything, by a sort of solemn sense of surrender to the empty passing of time."

This state is the state of letting go, in which the wisdom of the body is encouraged to mobilize itself.

As scientific work in altered states of consciousness (or ASC's) progresses, finer and finer distinctions are being made along the spectrum of consciousness. Dr. Stanley Krippner, who directs the dream laboratory at the Maimonides Medical Center in Brooklyn, has identified no fewer than twenty states, including dreaming, sleeping, hypnogogic, hypnopompic, hyperalert, lethargic, rapture, hysteria, fragmentation, regressive, meditative, trance, and so on.

Both the experimental psychologist and the anthropologist recognize that there are an extraordinary variety of paths to an ASC. Men may introduce into their bodies chemicals such as alcohol, LSD, heroin, mescaline, nicotine, or ether. They may dance like dervishes, go into the desert like hermits, be born again through an ordeal like the young braves among the Plains Indians, or see visions under conditions of extreme fatigue. They may listen to rock bands and see light shows. They may meditate, or pray, or practice one of the varieties of yoga, or enter a hypnotic state.

And this is not all, for investigators in this field have demonstrated a remarkable ingenuity in inventing devices to bring about an ASC. For example, Jean Houston and Robert

L. Masters, who direct the Foundation for Mind Research in New York, induce ASC's in experimental subjects by swinging them around in a sort of giant pendulum they call an ASCID, or Altered State of Consciousness Induction Device.

The blindfolded subject stands upright in a metal swing, held in by canvas bands. Responding to motions of the subject's body, the swing rotates, goes forward or backward, or moves from side to side. It takes as little as two minutes or as long as twenty minutes to induce the ASC.

Going into an ASC does not require any external agent at all. As Andrew Weil has pointed out, even young children appear to be driven by some inherent impulse to put themselves into an ASC when they whirl around and around until they fall to the floor in a state of consciousness quite different from the normal.

Hyperventilation (or breathing too rapidly and too deeply) is both a common symptom of anxiety and another common experiment by children who discover they can, without permanent harm, hyperventilate until they pass out. (Hyperventilation reduces the amount of carbon dioxide in the blood, causing it to become more alkaline and temporarily upsetting a delicate physiological balance.)

The ultimate objective of the more dedicated investigators into ASC's has been nothing less than to chart a path that will lead the traveler to the highest state of consciousness that man can reach, the state that Quakers call the Inner Light, that St. Paul called the peace that passeth understanding, that psychologist Abraham Maslow has called the peak experience, that Sufis call *fana*, Zen monks call *satori*, and yogis call *samadhi*.

The great German physicist Erwin Schrödinger, who understood things that are denied to most physicists, once wrote that "the mystics of many centuries, independently, yet in perfect harmony with each other (somewhat like the particles of an ideal gas) have described, each of them, the unique experience of his or her life in terms that can be described in the phrase: *Deus factus sum* (I have become God)."

In our exploration of altered states of consciousness we must necessarily stop short of finding the way to sainthood, salvation, or enlightenment in the classic sense. We are not trying to become gods.

Our interest is much more pragmatic and our starting point is the scientific investigation of the ASC's experienced by yogis in India and Zen masters in Japan.

## YOGA

Yoga represents one of the classic nonchemical means —probably *the* classic means—by which men can alter their consciousness, let go, and enter a state in which they can do things not possible when they are in the normal waking state.

It is now accepted as a fact that yogis can at will exercise control over some of the operations of their internal organs. Among the bodily functions they have shown they can control, even while wired up to laboratory instruments, are heart rate, blood pressure, and brain waves. To believe this requires no leap of faith, no conversion to Oriental mysticism, for these phenomena have been measured again and again.

The yoga most familiar to Westerners is hatha-yoga, or the "yoga of force," which trains the student to perform physical exercises, some of which require one to develop almost a contortionist's skill. Hatha-yoga is, however, quite a newcomer among the many varieties of yoga, which trace their origins to the great teacher Patanjali, who is believed to have lived in the second century B.C. Patanjali's yoga, which he summarized in his writings on the "eightfold path," became known as Raja yoga, or "royal yoga," and is concerned with training the spirit rather than the body. Of the other varieties of yoga, mantra-yoga—yoga that uses occult sounds —will be of the greatest interest to us because it is the basis of transcendental meditation.

Westerners first became interested in yoga in the 1700's, when army surgeons and other curious Britishers wrote home about having seen Indians who could survive such experiences as being buried alive for a matter of days or who could cause their hearts to stop beating. In the centuries since then yoga has been accepted by Westerners only grudgingly, being generally relegated to that half-world it shares with such other semi-respectable systems of belief as theosophy, health-foodism, extrasensory perception, and the cosmological theories of Immanuel Velikovsky.

To begin with, we find it hard to be comfortable with the pseudoscientific underpinnings of hatha-yoga. The theory of hatha-yoga is based upon *kundalini,* a divine power that is concentrated at the base of the spine. *Kundalini* is transmitted to six psychic centers by a vein that runs through the backbone. The supreme center is described as a lotus with a thousand petals located at the top of the skull. Salvation is reached when the yogi causes the *kundalini,* which is feminine, to rise through the vein in the backbone until it unites with the lotus with a thousand petals, which is masculine.

Such explanations of natural phenomena as this tend to embarrass us, even though in the end they are no more poetic than the commonly accepted theory of matter, which asks us to visualize the ultimate building blocks as atoms in which hard little balls called electrons whirl around a nucleus containing hard little balls called protons, in which a great deal of power is concentrated. Both theories happen to have some pragmatic value in explaining natural processes.

In any case yoga has, so to speak, been coming out of the closet in recent years. Notices for yoga classes appear on the bulletin board near the grocery where I shop. One class is held in the parish house of an Episcopalian church and the other in the town recreation hall.

Converts to yoga are many, and the recruits are sometimes unexpected. A year or so ago, a wire service distributed a memorable news photo of the eccentric Texas billionaire Haroldson Lafayette Hunt in a yoga *asana* or posture. Hunt, who is eighty-three, explained, "I was reading this book that explained how yoga can add ten or twenty years to your lifespan and I decided to take it up."

Few American scientists have shown a more enthusiastic

interest in the powers of yoga than Dr. Elmer Green, who heads the psychophysiological laboratory at the Menninger Foundation.

In 1969 Green, who had been working on the voluntary control of bodily functions, learned from a psychiatrist in St. Paul, Minnesota, of a forty-five-year-old yoga who had shown some remarkable abilities to control such bodily functions as the rate of his heartbeat. Green got in touch with Swami Rama and arranged for him to come to Topeka.

As Green describes the Swami's background, he had studied yoga since the age of four. He reached a prominent position in the yogic hierarchy of southern India, but renounced this in order to pursue learning. In 1969 he came to the United States when he was instructed by his guru to cooperate with scientists in an effort to bring the East and West closer together.

The investigators at the Menninger Laboratory wired up the Swami to a cardiotachometer, which recorded his heart rate, a gauge that recorded his breathing, and thermistors that measured his skin temperature.

In the course of the three days he spent at the lab, the most extraordinary powers that Swami Rama demonstrated had to do with his heart rate, which he increased and decreased at will. When he told Green that he could stop his heart for three minutes, Green answered a little nervously that ten seconds would be quite enough.

As it turned out, the experiment went on for seventeen seconds because of confusion in the control room and because the Swami had not in fact actually stopped his heart. But something equally interesting was going on.

The Swami had asked that the control room give him the signal "That's all" when he had succeeded in stopping his heart, but the signal was delayed while the men in the control room tried to make sense of what they saw on the polygraph paper. Instead of stopping, the Swami's heart rate had done quite the opposite and speeded up to about 300 beats per minute. Deciding that this must be what they had been waiting for, somebody said, "That's all," and the Swami established what he called a "solar plexus lock" to keep his heart in this state. (What he did is probably what physiologists call the "Valsava maneuver." The pressure inside the chest is increased by holding the breath and simultaneously straining downward.)

The Swami had not literally stopped his heart but had put it into a condition known as "atrial flutter." In this state the heart stops pumping blood and the pulse become undetectable. For practical purposes, the heart is no longer functioning. The Swami explained afterward that if he had maintained the "solar plexus lock," he could have kept his heart from functioning for several minutes.

Dr. Green and his wife, Alyce, and their colleagues are not the only scientists who have wired yogis up to recording devices. In the early 1960's three Indian scientists, B. K. Anand, G. S. Chhina, and B. Singh recorded the electrical activity in the brains of four yogis engaged in meditation. The EEG tracings showed well-marked alpha activity as they meditated. (Alpha waves are associated with deep relaxation.) As the yogis entered the state of inward-turning attention called *samadhi,* the alpha waves tended to be replaced by slower theta waves.

The yogic state is attained by intense concentration. Anand and his colleagues reported that they could not distract the yogis from meditation by banging gongs, flashing lights or holding hot test tubes against their skin. In their first report on Swami Rama the Greens described his technique as one of holding the breath while focusing attention, all without motion.

The control of breathing is a central element of the technique of yoga—more central even than the exercises and asanas we associate with yoga. There is a good physiological reason for the importance assigned to breathing, for our breathing is the one vital function we can control either voluntarily or involuntarily. Most of the time our autonomic nervous system is in charge of our breathing, which goes on without any conscious control, but we can shift without effort to the voluntary motor pathway and breathe deliberately.

*Prana,* or the discipline of breathing, is based on the belief that there is a connection between breathing and mental states. In particular slow and rhythmical breathing allows the practitioner to enter into mental states he could not otherwise reach. The ranking scholar of yoga, Professor Mircea Eliade, has described the phenomenon in these words: "Motionless, breathing rhythmically, eyes and attention fixed on a single point, the yogin experiences a passing beyond the secular modality of existence."

The Indians were not the only people to recognize the importance of breathing in meditative practices. The Chinese Taoist philosophers Lao-tzu and Chuang-tzu were both familiar with what they called "methodical respiration," while a Chou dynasty inscription of the sixth century B.C. describes respiratory techniques. Methodical breathing found its way to Japan in the form of Zen breathing exercises.

We have also learned how yogic breathing has been applied to modern hypertensive therapy by Dr. Datey in his Bombay hospital.

Old H. L. Hunt has often been right about the vagaries of the oil market. It appears highly likely that he is also right about the life-prolonging effects of yoga.

## SURVIVAL MANUAL: LESSON ONE

First we are going to record three physiological functions that are easy to measure. Then we will learn a yoga exercise that has been used successfully in an Indian hospital to reduce tensions in patients suffering from high blood pressure.

### Establishing a Baseline

In order to know how far you've gone, you have to know where you started from.

Before he starts an experiment, a physiologist will establish baselines against which he can measure his results. Each experimental subject, whether it is a rat, a monkey, or a human being, will have its own baseline, or perhaps many baselines, each one measuring a different function.

Before trying the exercises in survival techniques, you should establish a baseline against which you can measure your progress in learning how to let go.

The laboratory measurement of baselines may include such measurements as heart pressure, respiration, urine production, cardiac output, skin resistance, heart rate, and arterial blood gas analysis. Some of these measurements call for highly sophisticated equipment. Some do not.

We are going to establish three important baselines that can be measured with a minimum of equipment—a watch and a dime-store thermometer. The stress you are under is reflected in your heart rate, your rate of breathing, and your skin temperature. You can measure each of these yourself.

Ideally you should set aside a week to establish your baseline. It should, of course, be a normal week, which is to say you shouldn't be suffering from the flu or from an unusual amount of stress. Measure the three functions at the same time each day. It should be the same time at which you plan to do your exercises in letting go. (I find before breakfast to be the most convenient time myself, but when I have suggested this to friends, some of them have reacted with horror.)

An example of how we are going to use the baseline is a chart (page 83) of my skin temperature, measured before and after I started meditating. The solid line is the baseline, measured at seven each morning for seven days before I started meditating. The dotted line represents the measurements made for seven days *after* I started meditating. Clearly meditating made a difference in the temperature of my skin and presumably in the way in which I was handling stress.

## SKIN TEMPERATURE

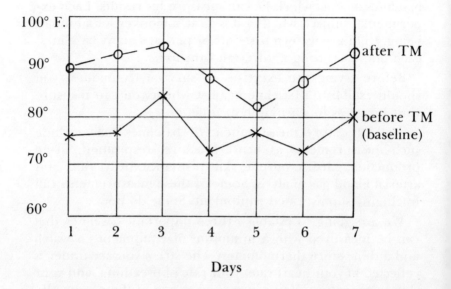

Days

To measure your heart rate, first of all sit down and relax. Take a few deep breaths. Make sure you have a watch or a clock with a second hand in a position where you can look at it. With the middle finger of your right hand, find the pulse in your left wrist. (Vice versa, if you're left-handed.)

When the second hand of your watch is at 0, start counting your pulse. Count for a full minute. Your heart rate will be affected by the time of day, whether or not you have just eaten, any recent excitement, and a host of other factors. It probably will not be below 60 and not above 90 beats a minute. Whatever it is, record it on the chart below with an X. Repeat this measurement every day at the same time for a week.

When you have recorded your heart rate, you will measure your respiratory rate. Sit quietly and relax for a moment. When the second hand of your watch touches 0, start counting each breath. Try to let your body do the breathing for you. Continue counting for three minutes. It will seem like a long time.

Heart Rate

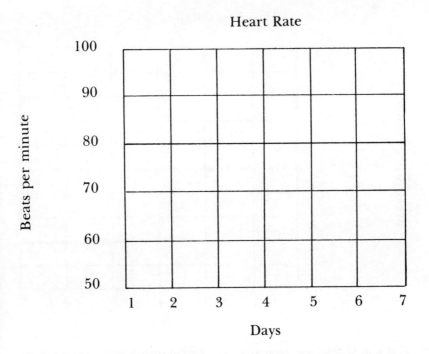

When the three minutes is up, divide your total count by three. The normal respiratory rate is usually about 15 breaths per minute, but, like the heart rate, this differs from person to person and, also like the heart rate, it changes with circumstances. Your rate will probably not be below 10 nor above 20.

Counting your breathing for three minutes is in fact a pretty effective exercise in letting go. You'll probably find that you were breathing somewhat more slowly during the last minute than you were at the beginning. Counting breaths is in fact an exercise practiced by Zen monks.

Record your rate on the table on page 86 and continue for a week.

After you have recorded your heart rate and your respiratory rate, you will measure and record your skin temperature, taken at the end of a finger. The temperature of your hand is an indicator of stress. (In a later survival lesson

Respiratory Rate

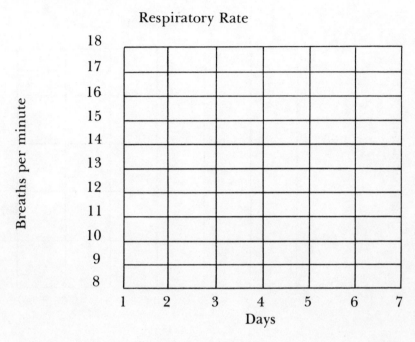

you will learn how to warm up your hands when you want to ward off feelings of tension or a headache.)

You will need an oral thermometer, the old-fashioned kind in which the temperature is measured by the height of a column of colored liquid inside a glass tube. (The one I bought cost ninety-eight cents.) If the glass bulb is exposed so that you can touch it, so much the better. If it isn't, carefully break away or cut away a piece of the plastic backing so that you can touch a finger to the bulb.

To measure your finger temperature, put the thermometer flat on a table in front of you. Touch the bulb with the ball of your index finger or your middle finger. (Always use the same finger of the same hand.) Keep your finger firmly on the bulb until the column of liquid stops moving. Record the temperature on the chart below. (If you are particularly relaxed, you may find that as you sit with your finger on the thermometer bulb, the temperature reading will tend to go higher and higher. This is good. Your hands are warming up spontaneously, a feedback effect we shall discuss later.)

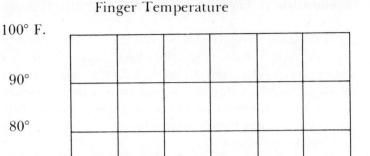

Finger Temperature

Now you are ready to try your first exercise in letting go.

## Shavasan

In the mid-1960's Dr. K. K. Datey and his colleagues at the K.E.M. Hospital in Bombay discovered that a yoga breathing exercise called "Shavasan" worked effectively to reduce headaches, giddiness, nervousness, irritability, and insomnia among patients suffering from hypertension. The exercise also reduced their mean blood pressure by an average of twenty-seven millimeters. Their heart rates dropped, and their respiratory rates went as low as four per minute.

Whether or not your blood pressure is higher than it should be—and it probably is—Shavasan is a first-rate exercise in letting go. Furthermore, it is easy and it is pleasant.

Take off your necktie, your shoes, or any other constricting clothing. Lie down on a bed or couch big enough to stretch out on. Lie on your back with your legs sprawling apart and your arms lying easily beside you but not touching your body. (Dr. Datey says that your legs should be spread at an angle of 30° and your arms at 15°.)

Close your eyes, not squeezing them shut, but letting your

eyelids droop. Let your fingers lie in a natural, half-curled position.

Dr. Datey instructed his patients to breathe regularly, breathing with their stomachs rather than with their chests. They were told to learn to breathe rhythmically in such a way that each inhalation was followed by a pause and each exhalation by a longer pause. This can be achieved by breathing to a slow count of seven, like this:

One, two—inhale
Three—hold
Four, five—exhale
Six, seven—hold
One, two—inhale again.

You should soon fall into such a regular rhythm of breathing that you hardly need to count. Counting, however, will keep your mind aware of what is going on in your body and will protect you from the intrusion of disturbing thoughts from the world outside. If you find you are breathing regularly without counting, think of the coolness of the air as it enters your nostrils and the warmth of the air as it leaves. (Unless you have a cold, always breathe through your nostrils rather than your mouth.) Imagine that your arms and legs are becoming heavier and heavier and warmer and warmer. Then go back to the seven count.

Dr. Datey's patients practiced Shavasan for thirty minutes a day. You should do it for at least twenty minutes a day. When you are through, measure your heart rate, breathing rate, and finger temperature, and compare them with your baseline measurements.

At the beginning you may find that there is no change at all, or even that the change is in the wrong direction. Don't be surprised or discouraged. Shavasan needs practice. The Indian patients took about three weeks to learn the exercise properly.

Of one group of ten Indian patients, nine showed improvement after they had been trained in Shavasan. The odds are nine to one that it will help you too.

## ZEN

To most of us yoga means difficult bodily contortions and deep breathing, while Zen means intellectual puzzles and carries with it a vaguely literary air. This latter characteristic was largely established when, at the height of his popularity, J. D. Salinger used a Zen *koan*—"What is the sound of one hand clapping?"—as the epigraph for one of his popular books.

In spite of their contrasting styles—yoga appears positively flamboyant when compared to the asceticism of Zen—the two systems have much in common, for each is essentially a pathway to enlightenment. If the word "enlightenment" embarrasses us, we may consider the goal simply as an ASC, or a letting go.

*Zen* is a Japanese word that means a state of absolute calmness and abstraction from this world. Like other prominent aspects of Japanese culture it is an import, having arrived from China, where it was called *ch'an.* The Chinese, in turn, had received *ch'an* from India, where it was called *dhyana,* or meditation.

Although technically a sect of Buddhism, Zen appears hardly religious to Christian or Jewish eyes, conditioned to equating religion with a belief in an omniscient and omnipotent god. Rather, Zen is a way of life whose goal is the attainment of a sense of internal peace called *satori.*

The great Zen teacher Daisetz Teitaro Suzuki has explained that "Satori may be defined as an intuitive looking into the nature of things in contradistinction to the analytical or logical understanding of it." He goes on to say that *satori* is "the opening of the mind-flower" or the "removing of the bar" or "the brightening up of the mind-works."

*Satori* is, in other words, not at all like salvation in the Christian sense but is instead the opening up of a profoundly new point of view, a point of view that is fed by the intuition rather than by the logical powers of the mind. It does not call for belief in any supernatural being.

The attainment of *satori* is generally a long and arduous process, carried out under the instruction of a Zen master in the training hall of a monastery. By tradition the novice arrives afoot, wearing a bamboo hat and straw sandals and is at first denied admittance. Only after he has pleaded to enter is he granted probationary status. After several more days he is allowed to join the community if he satisfies the master of his sincerity and dedication.

The course of training is painful, for the novices must sit motionless for hours at a time in the meditation hall. They do not kneel in the Japanese posture that has been easy and familiar to them since childhood, but sit cross-legged, in the "lotus posture," with their feet placed soles-up on their thighs. Their hands lie in their laps, the left hand uppermost, the thumbs touching. Their eyes are not shut. Instead they gaze at the floor.

While they meditate, monitors with sticks walk back and forth, eyes peeled for novices who have slipped off to sleep or have fallen into a bad posture. When they spot a transgressor, they bow politely before him and then beat him briskly on his shoulders with their wooden staves. The beaten novice is expected to thank the monitor politely.

The desired outcome of this fierce discipline is a state of pure meditation, which relieves the meditator of all distractions, both from the outer world and from the workings of the mind. The main thing, according to a notable passage written by Tai-hui, a twelfth-century Zen master, "is to shut off all your sense-organs and make your consciousness like a block of wood. When this block of wood suddenly starts up and makes a noise, that is the moment you feel like a lion roaming about freely with nobody disturbing him, or like an elephant that crosses a stream not minding its swift current."

The intellectual component of Zen, which has appealed to many intellectuals, is paradoxically, profoundly anti-intellectual. The style of Zen is not to reason or to argue but to know by direct intuition. Or, as the late Alan Watts once put it, "Direct pointing . . . is the open demonstration of Zen by nonsymbolic actions or words, which usually appears to the uninitiated as having to do with the most ordinary secular affairs, or to be completely crazy."

The literature of Zen is consequently puzzling to Westerners, for it is often completely foreign to what we like to consider to be the logical processes of thinking. My favorite Zen story is not, however, hard to understand at all.

The story goes that two Zen monks, while traveling, came to a swollen river on the bank of which an extraordinarily pretty young woman stood in distress, afraid to cross the tumbling river. The first monk, much to his companion's disapproval, promptly invited the girl to ride across the river on his back. He knelt, and the girl hitched up her rich kimono, revealing slender calves and ankles, and climbed aboard. When they had safely reached the other side without even wetting her kimono, the girl got off, thanked the monk prettily, and went on her own way while the two monks went on theirs.

That evening, over a bowl of rice gruel at a temple where they had found shelter, the second monk upbraided his friend for his kind deed. If the pretty young girl had been an ugly old woman, it might have been all right, but it was wicked to have placed himself in a position where his flesh might have been tempted. Not only had the girl revealed her shapely legs, but she had wrapped her arms and legs tightly around the monk while he took her through the torrent. The puritanical monk went on and on until he ran out of reasons why it had been a rash and dangerous thing to do. When he was through, his patient friend said merely, "I left that girl on the bank of the river. You're still carrying her on your back."

More typical of the style of Zen, which its practitioners call directness and which others find remarkably oblique, is a famous brief sermon preached by the master Jimyo.

"As soon as one particle of dust is raised, the great earth manifests itself there in its entirety," Jimyo told the congregation. "In one lion are revealed millions of lions, and in millions of lions is revealed one lion. Thousands and thousands of them there are indeed, but know ye just one, one only." He lifted up his staff and concluded, "Here is my own staff, and where is that one lion?"

When one tries to learn more about Zen, one is confronted by puzzling stories such as this, and by the Four Great Statements that sum up the religious content of Zen:

A special transmission outside the Scriptures.
No dependence on words and letters.
Direct pointing to the soul of man.
Seeing into one's nature and the attainment of Buddhahood.

The final aim of Zen is to arrive at a state of nothingness, the state called *satori* in Japanese. It is an experience that is said to reach into the deepest places of the mind and to bring about a reconstruction of the world.

Pure Zen does not have any practical worldly applications. It is done for itself and not for any desirable consequences it may bring. Yet, as we shall see, it is clear that desirable consequences often do follow the practice of Zen. Some of these have become apparent in the experiences of those Japanese, not monks, who have subjected themselves to Zen training. These have included, notably, warriors of the samurai class, who developed parallels between Zen and such martial arts as swordsmanship and archery. In practice Zen becomes a way of life in which things are allowed to happen naturally, without strain. The Zen archer, for example, does not strain to hit the target, but lets the arrow find its own way to the bull's-eye.

The mastery of Zen also appears to bring some benefits in the form of a long life, if one can trust the birth and death dates of four ancient Zen masters: Hui-hai (ninth century) lived to be ninety-four; Hsüeh-teng (tenth century) lived to be eighty-six; Eisai (thirteenth century) lived to be seventy-four; and Ingen (seventeenth century) lived to be eighty-one.

What goes on in the Zen master's body while he meditates? Two researchers at Tokyo University reported in 1966 that they had found regular variations during meditation in the electrical activity of the brain, the pulse rate, respiration, and the galvanic skin response. (The latter, usually abbreviated GSR, is a measure of the electrical resistance of the skin and is interpreted as an indicator of stress.)

These findings were made by Drs. Akira Kasamatsu and Tomio Hirai, who worked with the priests and disciples of two Zen sects. In age the subjects ranged from twenty-four to seventy-two. Their experience of Zen ranged from one year to twenty years.

EEG recordings made by Kasamatsu and Hirai both in the monastery and in the laboratory showed that the Zen state is characterized by the appearance of alpha waves (indicating relaxation) followed in the most experienced practitioners by theta waves (indicating a state of reverie). As we have already seen, the same results were also found with yogis.

Additional physiological changes have been reported by other investigators. After reviewing the scientific studies of Zen that have been carried on in Japan, Dr. Y. Akishige of Kyushu University reported there is general agreement that during Zen meditation the rates of breathing and of oxygen consumption decrease, the GSR becomes lower, and there is a slight increase in the pulse rate and the pH, or alkalinity, of the blood.

Considered physiologically, Zen is a means to let go and allow the body to put itself into a state of profound and strainless relaxation.

Psychological changes cannot be measured as easily as physiological changes. There is much evidence, however, that Zen, like yoga, brings with it many psychological benefits. Among these are not only the ability to enter an ASC of deep relaxation but also the acquisition of a more realistic view of the world as it is and not as we imagine it to be.

Erich Fromm, the distinguished psychoanalyst, has described enlightenment as a state in which the person as a whole is completely in tune with both internal and external reality. "He who awakes is open and responsive because he has given up holding onto himself as a thing, and thus has become empty and ready to receive," Fromm says. "To be enlightened means the full awakening of the total personality to reality."

Although Zen is only accidentally a system of healing, its clinical value in psychotherapy has been demonstrated in Japan. This application seems to have grown historically from the success that the monks had with mentally disturbed travelers who wandered into their monasteries and who were obliged to conform to the strict rules of the place.

A Japanese psychiatrist, Dr. Shomei Morita, has incorporated elements of Zen into a system of treatment for neurotics. The principles of Morita therapy, as it is known, are to combat egocentricity and bring the patient back into harmony with nature. The patient is encouraged to accept his illness in complete solitude and then brought back into society in gradual stages.

In practice Morita puts his patients to bed for as long as a week, forbidding them to see either other patients or even their therapist. They are left completely alone and are not allowed to read or write, smoke, telephone, or watch television. As Dr. Ilza Veith of the University of California Medical Center describes this solitary confinement, "The patient is left alone with his illness until he and his illness become one—he has to accept his illness in complete solitude."

Following this rest cure, the patient is encouraged to work in the hospital garden, and is reintroduced to society in the form of his fellow patients, the hospital staff, and the therapist. He keeps a diary, which is checked daily by the therapist, who discourages entries that harp on illness and self-importance and encourages entries that show progress toward what is considered to be a healthy reintegration into society.

Morita therapy is thoroughly in accord with the traditional values of Japanese society. Whether it would work equally well—or work at all—for individualized and urbanized Americans is so far a question to which there is no answer.

As techniques of letting go, both Zen and yoga appear to be well-suited to the prevention and relief of stress. They both induce profound relaxation. They both are accompanied by physiological changes that act to relieve stress. They have both been shown to be of value in treating sick people. The only difficulty is that nobody has found a way to teach Zen and yoga without many years of training.

Given the American passion for quick results, it should not surprise us that the most successful system of meditation in the United States can be practiced successfully after only four hours of training.

## TRANSCENDENTAL MEDITATION

In 1969 Dr. Demetri Kanellakos, a senior research engineer at the Stanford Research Institute in Menlo Park, California, had to admit to himself that he was living under stress that was becoming increasingly hard to bear.

"It was coming out of everything—job, family, emotional immaturity—a lot of stress," he told me in a recent conversation. "I started going to Esalen, down at Big Sur, and that was good for the weekend, but coming back I couldn't use it. It was strange to my environment because it was so drastically different from what I was doing. Besides, it was taking too much time and it was expensive.

"Then I went to hear a lecture about transcendental meditation, and I was initiated. I expected stars to sparkle and things to happen and to hear strange noises, and none of this happened. I was disappointed. But the next day I found myself going to the office a couple of hours earlier than usual. Somehow I'd got up feeling refreshed. And I finished my work a couple of hours earlier than usual.

"Somehow, I was working more efficiently. Instead of worrying about how I was going to finish all this work, I just sat down and finished it up. As I went on with TM, this continued to improve, and then I began to notice physiological and psychological changes. My pulse would change while I was meditating and my attitude would change. I thought some of these changes ought to be measurable."

Kanellakos is an intense, dark man who wears black horn-rims and combs his untidy hair toward his forehead as if to cover a bald spot. He uses his hands freely, and, as he recalled a past reverse, his eyes narrowed. "But when I attempted to persuade the life sciences department of SRI to look into this for the cause of science, I was very gently put in my place," Kanellakos went on. (His own field is ionospheric radio propagation.) "So when I saw that they were dragging their feet, I wrote a proposal and said we ought to verify some of the stuff we'd been reading about.

"Okay, we decided to have an experiment to test the teachability of TM to people who'd never heard of it, or who'd said they certainly wouldn't be caught doing it, or who thought it meant shaving your head and wearing a white sheet and living in a cave and withdrawing from the world.

"When we designed the project, none of the psychologists and neurophysiologists at SRI wanted to be head of it because they didn't want to put their reputations on the line," Kanellakos said. His eyes widened and his voice changed as he impersonated his reluctant colleagues. *"What's this creepy thing you're interested in? What's this creepy, spooky thing?"*

Kanellakos' face went back to normal and he shrugged. "So I became project leader. When the results began to look good, I withdrew."

All the results of the SRI study have not yet been published, but the available conclusions support the argument that transcendental meditation is both psychologically and physiologically different from merely relaxing with one's eyes closed while one mentally repeats a meaningless word. Yet this is all that transcendental meditation really is.

My own experience with TM began a couple of years later than had Demetri Kanellakos'. I'd become interested in TM while doing the research for this book and decided that I obviously couldn't write about it with any authority unless I tried it myself. I approached TM as a thorough skeptic. I am still a skeptic so far as the Maharishi Mahesh Yogi and his movement are concerned. Against this skepticism I have to place my own experience, which is that TM works—which is to say that it is one of several ways I have found of successfully letting go.

I became involved with TM by following the instructions in a poster advertising the weekly TM meetings that take place in the suburban county where I then lived. When I arrived, there were thirty or forty people sitting on undertakers' chairs in the living room of the house that serves as the local headquarters of the movement.

Although there were a few young longhairs present, I was surprised to see that most of the people there for the first of two free lectures were in their forties and fifties. Some of them were considerably older. They gave an impression of great earnestness.

Our instructor was a dark, balding young man of about thirty-five, who wore a neat, tan, mod suit and a fashionably wide tie. He sat down on a bench in front of us and apologized for being late. He introduced himself (I'll call him Fred) and said that before he'd joined the movement full-time he'd been an engineer.

On the mantel behind Fred hung a rather garish painting of two East Indians. The man in the foreground—squat, dark, long-haired, benign—was, Fred told us, Maharishi himself. The ethereal figure behind him was Guru Dev, Maharishi's spiritual master.

During the lecture that followed and its sequel the next week, Fred delivered a well-organized and well-rehearsed presentation of what TM is and what it is not. Fred told us that TM is not a religion but a meditative practice, a natural technique that, in Maharishi's words (people in the movement never say *the* Maharishi) "allows the conscious mind to experience increasingly more subtle states of thought until the source of thought, the unlimited reservoir of energy and creative intelligence, is reached." Consequently, Fred told us, it was a means by which each of us could learn to use his full potential. TM was, furthermore, a natural and easy way to allow the body to enter a state of rest resembling the deepest stage of sleep.

Fred went on to declare that TM was a means of solving the drug problem, bringing tranquility on the domestic scene, achieving international peace, and promoting harmony between the various races. (At this point I looked around the room and noted that there weren't any blacks present.)

During the question period somebody asked Fred how one could be sure that he could learn TM. Anybody could learn TM, Fred answered. I objected, saying that I just couldn't believe they'd never had a failure. Fred looked me straight in the eye and repeated that the movement had never had a failure. Not *one* in the history of TM? Not one, Fred said.

I didn't particularly like Fred and didn't believe that TM had never failed, but I decided to go back to the next meeting anyway.

Fred, who was wearing the same neat suit with a new tie, quickly got down to more particular things. He described to us the findings of a Harvard physiologist named Wallace, who had established that TM produces a state of consciousness that is quite distinct from sleep or a hypnotic trance and that promotes a state of profound relaxation. Studies of meditators in Wallace's laboratory had demonstrated that the metabolism slows down, the heart rate decreases, the brain goes into the alpha state, and so on.

Leaving these scientific findings, Fred sketched a picture on a newsprint pad to illustrate what Maharishi meant when he said that TM systematically takes the mind of the meditator to the source of thought, the pure field of creative intelligence. The picture looked like this:

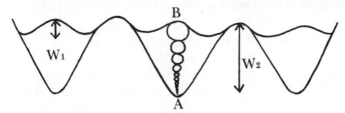

Fred explained that turning the attention inward takes the mind from experiencing a thought at the conscious level (point B) to finer and finer and more and more subtle states of thought until the mind arrives at A, which is the source of thought. The consciousness expands during the process from $W_1$ to $W_2$.

Less formally, Fred explained, TM allows one to use one's mantra to dive down to where the tiny bubbles of conscious thought originate. Twenty minutes later one comes back up, rested, relaxed, and at peace with the world. (The mantra is a meaningless word that the meditator repeats to himself while he meditates.)

A spry, white-haired lady asked how TM could accomplish in two lectures and an initiation—about four hours—the same results that the yogi and the Zen adept took many years to accomplish. Fred answered that TM took advantage of a natural capacity of the mind, and that the technique was simply a matter of finding the line of least resistance.

She then asked if TM was useful in an emergency that threatened to throw one into a state of psychic panic. Fred shook his head. "As Maharishi says," he told us, smiling, "TM isn't a Band-Aid to be applied at times of stress throughout the day. Twice a day we drown ourselves in meditation. The rest of the day we drown ourselves in action."

While he was talking, I noticed a curious thing about Fred. He had a nervous habit of rubbing his cheekbone just under his right eye. He looked quite calm otherwise, but every minute or two his right hand went up and his index finger massaged the cheekbone. I wondered about TM and stress.

Yet, when Fred invited those of us who wanted to be initiated to stay behind, I decided to go ahead with it. After I'd filled out a form Fred instructed me to present myself on Saturday morning at ten o'clock for my initiation. He advised me to eat only a very light breakfast, preferably nothing at all, and to bring some fresh fruit, half-a-dozen flowers, a brand-new handkerchief, and a check for seventy-five dollars.

I don't know if it's significant or not, but I had a terrible time sleeping on Friday night. My mind was racing away in all directions. My heart was beating too fast. I tried some homemade meditation to slow myself down (I'd been experimenting with meditation), but it didn't work. My mind continued to shoot off thoughts like a roman candle. I fell asleep at last and overslept in the morning.

After a fast cup of coffee, I picked a couple of hydrangeas and some geraniums from the garden and stopped at a shopping center, where I bought a cheap handkerchief at the five-and-dime and three nectarines at the market.

At the meditation center, a good-looking girl named Roberta, whom I'd seen at the lectures, told me what a pretty bunch of flowers I'd brought and asked me to take off my shoes. I did. I filled out another form while Roberta took my offerings into an adjoining room. When she came back, she asked me to make out a check for seventy-five dollars, and I did.

Fred was waiting for me in the adjoining room. He was sitting in a comfortable chair to one side of an altar, and he was wearing his favorite mod suit. The altar consisted of a table on which were a couple of brass bowls that looked as if they'd come from India. One held water, and the other my nectarines. My handkerchief was lying on the table, as were the flowers. A stick of incense burned in a holder. On the wall behind the altar hung a deplorable picture of the Maharishi.

Fred invited me to sit down in another overstuffed chair. He welcomed me and said I would find what we were going to do to be absolutely natural and undemanding and asked me to follow his instructions in the easiest and most natural way.

Before we began the initiation, Fred said, he'd like me to take part in a little ceremony. He took one of the hydrangeas and gave me a geranium. We stood up together in front of the altar and the picture of the Maharishi.

Fred dipped the hydrangea in the bowl of water and shook it toward the picture. Then he began to sing a monotonous little song that sounded vaguely East Indian to me. The song went on for a while, and then without an intermission Fred began to chant a meaningless syllable. He turned to me and gestured that I should join him. The two of us chanted in unison. I now knew that this word, which I promised not to reveal, was my mantra. Fred pointed to the chairs. We sat down and I closed my eyes and said my mantra more and more quietly until at last I was saying it silently to myself.

As I sat there saying my mantra to myself, I was conscious of two things. First, saying the mantra over and over didn't absolutely clear my mind of thoughts, but it went a long way toward it. Every time a thought broke through, I could get rid of it by going back to the mantra. I couldn't hold a thought and the mantra at the same time, and the mantra always won in the end. The thoughts came and went, but the mantra went on and on.

The second thing of which I became aware was that my body was becoming entirely relaxed. My hands lay loosely in my lap, and my head sank down toward my chest. I was as loose as an unstrung guitar. It felt wonderful.

The time went by quite fast, and I was surprised when I heard Fred saying, "Open your eyes very slowly. Stretch. Take your time. Don't rush."

I followed his instructions and finally opened my eyes all the way.

"Now," Fred said, "you've been initiated into transcendental meditation."

I was speechless. I mean I sat there and stared at Fred and

either couldn't say anything or didn't want to. Finally, reluctantly, I said, "Oh, yes."

We discussed my experience for a few minutes, particularly the sense of letting go completely and the attempted intrusion of unwanted thoughts. Fred seemed quite pleased. He told me not to worry about the thoughts, that Maharishi said each thought was a sign that stress had been relieved somewhere in the body. The more thoughts, the more stresses were being relieved. Fred told me that whenever a thought intruded I should just go back to the mantra and the thought would go away. He cautioned me, however, against trying to force the mantra.

Roberta came in and took me to another room, where she told me to meditate alone for another ten minutes or so. Afterward she asked me to fill out a questionnaire about my experience with TM. I wrote that while I was meditating my body had felt like a log.

Now comes the most extraordinary part of my experience with TM. Roberta gave me back my handkerchief and one of the nectarines, and I put my shoes back on and walked out of the center and onto the street, eating the nectarine as I went. I knew that something most remarkable had happened to me. The only proper description of what went through me during the first few moments is contained in an old and overused expression: I felt as if I'd been born again.

The sunlight seemed brighter than it had before. The colors of the trees and of the cars driving by and of the clothes of the people I passed all seemed more intense. The air seemed cleaner and more invigorating. The nectarine tasted sweeter. I felt as if it were the first day of spring after a long, cold, gray winter. I felt like a child who has been given an unexpected and much-wanted holiday. The world was a beautiful place, and I was part of it.

As a professional skeptic, I find it rather embarrassing to have to bear testimony to the effectiveness of transcendental meditation. I was, consequently, rather relieved when I picked up an issue of our county weekly and found that its publisher, a wry, humorous, civilized man named Steve McNamara, had also been initiated and also felt embarrassed at having to bear public witness that TM worked.

"I feel a hell of a lot better than I did before I started meditating," McNamara reported. "I'm more relaxed. I snap less at my friends and my kids. I smile more. I experience a lot less anxiety, anguish, despair—emotions associated with the treadmill lives most of us live."

McNamara argues that the initiation fee of seventy-five dollars is set rather arbitrarily. "It is worth either $7.50 or $7,500. Only $7.50 if the thing doesn't work for you and all you've gotten is some cocktail party conversation. The value is closer to $7,500 if, as if with me, the thing works."

One can only consider the Maharishi skeptically, for his public life has included some curious and diverting episodes. The Maharishi burst onto the general consciousness of the world in the 1960's, when he was adopted by the Beatles, who took up TM as an alternative to using drugs. In the winter of 1968 the four singers, accompanied by wives and girlfriends, took up residence at the Maharishi's ashram in the foothills of the Himalayas.

Ringo Starr defected during the second week, but the others stayed on, meditating and apparently absorbing serenity and wisdom from the Maharishi, a bearded, smiling figure who speaks fluent, Indian-accented English and often ends a sentence with a little chuckle.

The publicity brought other musicians and actors to the ashram: the Rolling Stones and their epicene leader, Mick Jagger; Donovan, the singer; a group called the Beach Boys; and the actresses Shirley MacLaine and Mia Farrow. The show-business era of transcendental meditation ended when the Maharishi embarked on an ill-advised concert tour of the United States, accompanied by the Beach Boys. When the tour came unglued, the Maharishi went back to India, where he bided his time.

The Maharishi's origins are shrouded in appropriate mystery. His biographers say that he was born in 1918, the son of a forest ranger. He is said to have graduated from Allahabad University with a degree in physics, but instead of following a conventional career in the great world, he came under the influence of Swami Brahmananda Saraswati, or Guru Dev, a prominent religious leader with whom he spent thirteen years. Before his death, Guru Dev is said to have charged the Maharishi with the mission of developing a form of meditation simple enough to be practiced by anybody.

The Maharishi is said to have discovered TM during two years of solitary living in the Himalayas. Back in the world of men he embarked in the mid-1950's on his great mission. Apart from such setbacks as the Beach Boys tour, the TM movement, together with its twin, the Science of Creative Intelligence (SCI), has flourished like the proverbial bay tree.

In 1972 the movement consciously directed itself toward a goal so ambitious that it calls into serious question the good sense of the responsible leaders.

The year 1973 was announced to be the "Year of Action to Implement the World Plan." To start the year propitiously, the Maharishi observed a week of silence and then toured the United States, beating the drums for the Year of Action. He appeared on television, gave public lectures, and addressed the state legislatures of Illinois and Michigan. He met with the governors of these two states as well as the governors of Iowa and Georgia, and, according to a movement source, the governors became "inspired with his work and the great effect that the widespread adoption of TM is having on society."

Even granting the Maharishi's sincerity and the demonstrated value of TM to an apparent majority of its practitioners, it is hard to accept the main objective of the World Plan as the work of serious-minded men. It is nothing less than to provide a teacher of TM for every 1,000 people in the world. Given a world population of 3.7 billion, this calls for the training of 3,700,000 teachers. The course for meditators desiring to become teachers of TM costs $600. Thus, the

potential income from the training of teachers alone is over
$2 billion, which is somewhat larger than the net income of
General Motors in 1971.

Even leaving aside such eyewash for the faithful, the
worldly success of the TM movement is striking enough.
There are somewhere in the neighborhood of 300,000
meditators in the United States and the newsletters of the
Students International Meditation Society and the International Meditation Society—both of which are based in Los
Angeles—announced regularly that 16,000 new meditators
are being initiated each month.

The movement's greatest success has been on the college
campuses. Perhaps curiously—and perhaps not—it has
found some of its most fertile ground at such old-line institutions as Yale. When the Maharishi came to New Haven in
1966, he spoke to an overflow audience of students and faculty in Woolsey Hall; some months later the readers of the
usually staid *Yale Alumni Magazine* were treated to a love
letter to TM written by Al Rubottom, class of 1969, who has
been prominent in the movement's development in New England. (Ironically TM's Yale headquarters is in the office
formerly occupied by Students for a Democratic Society.)

. Rubottom's article was buttressed by a selection of personal testimonials from Yale meditators. Typical of these was
the statement of Sam Suffern, a biology instructor, who told
Rubottom: "There's been a quantum increase in the quality
of my life since I started meditation. I feel that the clarity of
my thinking, the enthusiasm with which I approach my
work, the amount of myself I can give to my students and
everyone I interact with, all have increased many times."

While the campuses have been the main seedbed for transcendental meditation, other meditators are found far from
the ivied walls. Joe Namath is a meditator. Sixty members of
the American Conservatory Theatre, San Francisco's reper-
tory company, were initiated and meditate daily. (The general director of the company reports, "I have perceived in
the company a greater clarity of mind, a lightness of spirit,

an increased efficiency and a sense of carefree creativeness.")
Nearly fifty California legislators, their staff members and
others who work at the capitol in Sacramento are meditators.
Surprisingly, one of these is the Roman Catholic chaplain of
the assembly, Father Leo McAllister. After he started
meditating, Father McAllister lost fifteen pounds and quit
smoking. "Whether it's meditation or not, I don't know," he
told a reporter, but he hasn't stopped.

Although the army has not yet adopted TM as a training
device, this is not due to any lack of meditators in uniform.
Their ranks range from the enlisted grades to a major general.

The major general is Franklin M. Davis, who in 1971 became commandant of the Army War College. Before this
appointment, while on temporary duty at the Pentagon waiting for a Vietnam-acquired infection to clear up, Davis came
across TM and decided to give it a try. He became a convert
when he found that his blood pressure had dropped ten
points and he had become generally immune to the horrors
of life in Washington.

After he became a prominent meditator General Davis
met the Maharishi in person at a symposium at Amherst,
Massachusetts. As Davis recalled the occasion: "I was taken to
his door, asked to remove my shoes, and escorted into his
hotel room. He was sitting on his mat, on a bed, his legs
carefully crossed.

"He shook my hand and said, 'How do you do, it's so nice
what you have done for us.'

"This sort of startled me. I didn't feel I had done anything."

The army has taken no official line on TM but has encouraged voluntary programs at a number of its installations.
Davis declares that he is totally convinced that TM could be
an effective means of coping with the army's drug problem.

"This system offers a reasonable approach for a youngster
to make the very difficult necessary adjustment between
himself and his new surroundings, from within," Davis told

the writer Jhan Robbins. "Personal stability has a great deal to do with keeping off drugs, and I think this is what TM can offer—this great stability."

I am myself put off by religious and semi-religious movements of all sorts and would find it satisfying to be in a position to suggest that the reported successes of TM are purely subjective. This would surely be enough, for it is a common observation that when we think we feel better, or more confident, or more alive, we in fact act more confidently and more positively. But this is not all, for a series of laboratory investigations at UCLA and Harvard have established that objective physiological changes go on in the body of the meditator.

The first public sign that scientists had become interested in TM came in the form of a letter published in the November 1969 issue of the prestige-laden *New England Journal of Medicine,* over the signature of Herbert Benson, M.D., of the Harvard Medical School.

Dr. Benson wrote to describe an experiment in which he had tested transcendental meditation as an alternative to drug abuse. Twenty volunteers had given up marijuana, barbiturates, LSD, amphetamines, and heroin after taking up TM. "All reported that they no longer took these drugs because drug-induced feelings became extremely distasteful as compared to those experienced during the practice of transcendental meditation," Benson wrote. "Perhaps transcendental meditation should be explored prospectively by others who are primarily interested in the alleviation of drug abuse."

Benson himself lost little time following up this promising lead with the help of a research associate at Harvard's Thorndike Laboratory, R. Keith Wallace, a physiologist who had written his doctoral dissertation at UCLA on the measurable bodily effects of TM. Wallace had also published an article in *Science* in 1970 that had sparked serious scientific interest in the subject.

At an international conference on drug abuse in 1971

Benson and Wallace reported on a broad study of TM as an effective answer to the problem of drug abuse. Their study was based on questionnaires sent to some 2,000 meditators, who had practiced TM an average of twenty months.

The results were well worth reporting. The great majority of the meditators reported that they had sharply decreased their use of drugs. Most of those who had meditated more than twenty-one months had stopped using drugs altogether. The most remarkable results were reported by the former users of hard narcotics. About 17 percent of the subjects had used hard narcotics, mainly heroin, before starting TM. After twenty-one months only 1.2 percent reported any use of narcotics at all, and all of these described themselves as light users.

The case was much the same among those who used more socially acceptable drugs such as hard liquor and cigarettes. The use of both dropped to a fraction of what it had been.

The use of drugs is a common response to psychological stress, and the mechanism is not hard to understand. Whether the person under stress turns to liquor, pot, or heroin, he enters a state of consciousness in which the stressor simply doesn't matter much anymore. The quarrel with his wife becomes less destructive, his financial situation seems less desperate, the chance of being fired less ominous, and the world in general seems a less threatening place. But when the user comes down from his high and back from his trip, the stressors are still there. He escapes by going on another trip.

If we are to accept these reports of former users, it seems clear that TM provides a useful alternative to drugs. To what extent this is a psychological mechanism and to what extent it may have a physiological basis is not yet clear. It is quite clear, however, that TM *does* have an extraordinary effect on certain physiological functions that can be measured in the laboratory.

The remarkable effect that TM has on such stress-related

bodily functions as heart rate, oxygen consumption, and brain waves was first measured and reported by Wallace in his doctoral dissertation. His observations and conclusions have been confirmed in his later work, carried out with Benson at the Thorndike Lab, an ancient brick and masonry building on the grounds of Boston City Hospital.

Sitting in a chair, each volunteer meditator extended his or her bare arm through a slit in a curtain. On the other side of the curtain, a catheter was inserted (after local anesthesia) in the subject's brachial artery, in order to take blood samples and to measure the blood pressure continuously. The subject was also wired up to recording instruments that measured heart rate, rectal temperature, skin resistance and the electrical activity of the brain. Measurements were made while the subject sat quietly before meditation, during meditation, and after meditation.

The results bore out the earlier reports that transcendental meditation produced physiological changes that are the opposite to those induced by stress.

The rate and volume of breathing became lower, dropping to about four to six breaths per minute. The amount of oxygen consumed fell by about 20 percent. There was a marked decrease in the level of blood lactate, whose presence is associated with stress. The heartbeat was slowed by about five beats per minute. The electrical resistance of the skin rose rapidly.

There was little change in the blood pressure during meditation, but at the same time it was observed that the average blood pressure of the meditators was unusually low. (The average was 106/57 mm.) The EEG patterns showed a relatively high activity of alpha waves.

Summing up, Wallace and Benson observed that the practice of TM seemed to put the meditator into a unique "wakeful, hypometabolic" state similar to that observed in yogis and Zen masters who had fifteen or twenty years of experience.

Wallace and Benson believe that TM has a direct clinical application to the problem of stress. As they put it, "During man's early history the defense-alarm reaction may well have had high survival value and thus have become strongly established in his genetic makeup. It continues to be aroused in all its visceral aspects when the individual feels threatened. Yet in the environment of our time the reaction is often an anachronism. Although the defense-alarm reaction is generally no longer appropriate, the visceral response is evoked with considerable frequency by the rapid and unsettling changes that are buffeting modern society. There is good reason to believe the changing environment's incessant stimulations of the sympathetic nervous system are largely responsible for the high incidence of hypertension and similar serious diseases that are prevalent in our society."

Benson and Wallace's results appear to be valid in spite of a recent development that is distressing from a purely scientific point of view. In 1972 Wallace left the Thorndike to accept the presidency of the Maharishi International University in California.

When I phoned Dr. Benson to ask if he had had any second thoughts about their joint work after Wallace's defection, he answered that he had personally monitored the experiments and was convinced of their validity. When I asked him if he was pursuing these investigations now, he answered a little starchily that he simply declined to discuss unpublished work and went on to make clear that he did not want to see me personally, for he was afraid that a visit to his lab might encourage me to publish some premature conclusions. I was disappointed but I was obliged to sympathize with him.

Benson is not the only medical-school researcher into transcendental meditation. When I visited Dr. Sydney G. Margolin at his human behavior laboratory at the University of Colorado, I found him not only willing to talk but also in a state of considerable animation. He had just made an observation that had excited him in the course of investigating the effects of TM on a pregnant girl."

Showing me a long sheet of polygraph paper that bore the characteristic peak-and-valley traces left by the recording pens, Margolin, who is a psychiatrist in his mid-sixties, explained that he had become interested in this young woman because she was planning to use TM as an anesthetic during the birth of her child.

"Not only were we intrigued by the idea of transcendental meditation," Margolin went on, "but we were intrigued by the idea that it will regulate processes by which pain is acknowledged. But this is not the point of the story. We were getting a baseline, using our equipment, and while we were examining her, we palpated the baby and I decided I was going to record the baby too, which I did."

Margolin's excitement came from his discovery that the peaks and valleys in the expectant mother's record were matched by peaks and valleys in the unborn baby's record.

"What came through," he told me, "was a unique experience for me in that the baby was obviously responding to what was going on in the conversation between the mother and me. And the baby was also responding to its mother's attempts at transcendental meditation."

I asked how Dr. Margolin thought the communication between the baby and the mother and the outside world took place. He told me he doubted it was a biochemical reaction, since this would have to be transmitted through the umbilical cord, requiring too long a time for the concentrations of the effective substances to build up. Instead he thought the unborn baby perceived something, that it had some sense perception on the order of hearing or touch.

Margolin commented in passing that many medical students at Colorado were practicing TM, forming a considerable community of meditators.

"We're going to see if we can replicate what other people [Benson and Wallace] have done," he told me. "We've already had differences in our observations—so we'll see. But that TM is a real phenomenon in terms of the subjective experience of the meditator goes without saying."

## SURVIVAL MANUAL: LESSON TWO

### Meditation

As we've already noted, there is simply no question that in spite of all the nonsense surrounding the Maharishi Mahesh Yogi, transcendental meditation works. It also requires a minimum of time and effort.

If you want to investigate transcendental meditation and don't know of a group near you, write to the headquarters of the International Meditation Society, 1015 Gayley Avenue, Los Angeles, California 90024.

For readers who mistrust the Maharishi and his followers or who don't care to risk seventy-five dollars, there are other roads to meditation. They are not inferior, but they call for more persistence and more patience. What is missing is the assurance that is brought by the teacher, the repeated statements that TM has never failed, the ceremonial initiation, and, I might add, the commitment to success that is made when you hand over your initiation fee.

It is not hard to learn to meditate without a teacher. The main thing is to come to the experience with positive expectations that you are going to succeed but without overblown notions of what is going to happen to you. You are, after all, mainly interested in meditation as a road to letting go of your tensions and not as a path to finding the secret of the universe.

Before I was initiated into TM, I had tried meditating on my own and thought I had failed. This was because I was expecting too much. After learning TM I realized that my earlier experience had been just as truly meditation. This is why, before I give instructions for meditation, I am going to describe my own experience.

Generally speaking meditating is not for me a particularly extraordinary or "transcendental" experience. It's just part of my day. Early in the morning I sit in a comfortable chair with the lights turned low. I sit upright with my neck straight, just as the Bhagavad Ghita recommends. Being something of a traditionalist, I place my hands in my lap in the Zen position, left hand lying in right palm, thumbs touching.

I breathe deeply several times. Then I close my eyes and begin saying my mantra in my mind. Other thoughts work their way in: Shall I pay the dentist's bill or let it ride until next month? Shall I rewrite that article or let it go and hope for the best? I don't fight the thoughts but merely go back to the mantra. Sometimes both the mantra and the thoughts vanish and I have a brief moment of nothingness. I have been told that this is what is meant by cosmic consciousness.

After the first few minutes I often find that I take a deep breath, almost a sigh. This is apparently a signal from my body that I am entering a different state, for my breathing immediately becomes slower and my sense of relaxation deeper. It is a very pleasant feeling.

After about fifteen minutes I begin to feel restive. After three or four more minutes, I open my eyes, stretch, turn up the light and begin my day's work. Almost always I feel a sense of well-being and cheerfulness.

Now and then I have had curious experiences while meditating. Sometimes I see a sort of light show, a play of light and dark shapes in my mind's eye. (Jhan Robbins has reported that when he was initiated into TM, his mantra appeared in his mind's eye, glowing like a huge neon sign. Alas, nothing this dramatic has ever happened to me.)

Several times I have had the hallucination that I am floating on air. I stop feeling the seat of the chair under my bottom and the carpet under my feet. A good-looking blond woman who was initiated the same morning I was told me later that her first experience took her completely out of her body.

In my early experience with meditation I always measured my heart and breathing rates and my finger temperature after meditating and compared it with my baseline measurements. My heart rate dropped, though not dramatically. My finger temperature went up markedly—often as much as ten degrees. My breathing also slowed down remarkably. I know this quite precisely because I have monitored it against the pulse I can hear in my ear while I meditate. Each complete respiration, in and out, takes about ten pulse beats. Conveniently my heart rate is usually about sixty beats per minute at that time in the morning. Thus, my breathing rate is about six per minute, or less than half my normal rate.

Meditating is extraordinarily simple.

First, find a quiet place where you won't be disturbed. (Later you will find that you can meditate anywhere. I have meditated in the Los Angeles airport during the evening rush and while lying on a cot at the blood bank.) At the beginning, however, the main thing is to be sure that you aren't going to be interrupted. It's hard not to feel self-conscious and nervous if there's a chance that somebody may blunder in and demand to know what you're doing.

Choose a mantra. I suggest that you use either OM, which is considered to be the supreme mystic syllable, or SHOM, which is also known to have considerable power. Other potent mantras are said to be AYN, HUM, and MU.

Posture is not particularly important so long as you are comfortable. The lotus posture is for other people. Sitting upright is perfectly acceptable and is in fact a yoga posture called the *maitreya asana*. Don't slump. Keep your back and neck upright.

Take two or three deep breaths, close your eyes, and begin to say the mantra over and over. Thoughts will spring to the surface of your mind. Whenever they do, go back to the mantra. That is all there is to it. Continue for twenty minutes or so, and in any case for not less than fifteen minutes. When you are through, open your eyes, breathe deeply, and stretch.

Don't be discouraged by the impression that nothing is happening. That is precisely the point: On the level of conscious thought, nothing *is* happening.

While nothing is happening in your mind, something measurable may be going on in your body. Take your heart rate, breathing rate and finger temperature after meditating. Record them day by day on the charts in Chapter 4. When your pulse and breathing slow down and your hands become warmer after meditating, you are well on the way. You have learned how to let go.

Some excellent advice for the beginning meditator has been offered by Chogyam Trungpa, a Tibetan monk who now lives in this country. "One must practice meditation without expectation or judgment and without thinking in terms of the future at all. Just leap into it. Jump into it without looking back. Just start on the technique without a second thought."

If you find it hard just to jump in and feel that you need some more instruction, you can still learn to meditate without going to a teacher.

If you don't own a tape recorder, beg or borrow one. It can be either a reel-to-reel machine or one of the small and popular cassette recorders. Then record in your own voice the following instructions on the tape. Read the instructions in a slow, firm, positive voice. Don't worry if you make a mistake. Just correct yourself and go on.

These instructions were developed at the University of Oregon by Terry V. Lesh and are based on work done by P. Wienpahl and Edward W. Maupin, researchers into altered states of consciousness. They have been used in carefully controlled experiments and have been shown to be effective in bringing about the meditation experience.

"Keep your back straight and erect; your hands in your

lap, the left palm facing inward on the right palm, with the tips of the thumbs touching. Your head too is erect, the ears on the plane of the shoulders, and the nose in line with the navel. You may keep your eyes closed or open as you prefer. If you have them open, fix them, unfocused, on the floor at a point about two or three feet in front of you. Now raise your whole body slowly and quietly, move it repeatedly to the left and to the right, forward and around, until you feel the best position.

"Breathe through your nose, inhaling as much as you need, letting the air come in by distending the diaphragm. Don't draw it in, rather let it come to you. Exhale slowly and completely, getting all the air out of your lungs. As you exhale slowly, count 'one.' Now inhale again, then exhale to the count of two. And so on up to ten. Then start over again with one and repeat up to ten again.

"You will find counting difficult as your mind will wander. Keep at it though, keep bringing your mind back to the process of counting your breath. As you become able to do the counting with reasonable success, start playing the following game with the counting. As you count one and are slowly exhaling, pretend that the 'one' is going down, down, down, into your stomach. Then think of its being down there as you inhale and begin to count two. As you exhale bring the 'two' down and place it in your stomach beside the 'one.' Eventually you will find that your mind itself, so to speak, will descend into your stomach.

"Gradually it will become possible for you to concentrate with more and more success on the numbers. Your mind will wander, and you will find yourself carried away on trains of thought, but it will become easier and easier to bring your mind back to the counting of your breath. Don't try to keep the 'alien' thoughts out. Instead just try to concentrate on the counting. You may take note of the thoughts as they come in, if necessary, and then return to the counting.

"You may find that you become anxious or uncomfortable. This is because sitting still and concentrating like this restricts the usual ways we have of avoiding discomfort. If you feel uncomfortable, just accept it. If you feel pleasant, accept that with the same indifference. Eventually you will be able to be quiet in both body and mind."

When you are through reading these instructions, let the tape run blank for twenty minutes. (Wienpahl and Maupin suggest half an hour, but my own experience is that this is a little too long.) When the twenty minutes is up, speak into the microphone again, saying, "Okay, the time is up. This meditation session is over. Take a deep breath and stretch."

Now rewind the tape. If you aren't already in a quiet, comfortable and private place, find one, taking the recorder with you of course. Start the tape going and do exactly as your own voice tells you to do.

Just jump in and don't look back.

# 4
# Letting Go with Hypnosis

## HYPNOSIS AND THE DOCTOR

IN THE BOARD room of the Toronto Rehabilitation Center, four men sit on a couch, eyes closed, heads back, hands lying loosely in their laps, relaxed. Their physician, Dr. E. Harvey Doney, tells them to visualize themselves in a lovely meadow. They are told to fill their lungs with fresh air, drawing it in "through your whole body and reaching your heart." Doney's voice drones on, telling them to imagine they are exercising, jogging.

Each of the men has had at least one heart attack. They are part of an experiment comparing the merits of hypnosis and exercise in rehabilitating victims of heart attacks. Elsewhere in the building another group of men is actually jogging under the supervision of another doctor. The joggers receive no hypnosis, while the men undergoing hypnosis do no exercise.

At the end of the first year of this experiment, to the surprise of both the doctors and the patients themselves, there was no significant difference between the two groups. The EKG readings of the men were so alike that not even a cardiologist could tell which man had been jogging and which man had been doing hypnosis.

"We aren't trying to disprove the claim made by those who advocate exercise," Dr. Terence Kavanaugh, director of the center, told a reporter from *Medical World News*. "But it seems to us that there is a missionarylike zeal among those who believe in its healing powers." Kavanaugh and his colleagues did in fact expect the exercise group to come out on top after the first year, and the initial results seemed to bear out this expectation. But soon both groups reached a plateau, and after that it was even stephen.

The study is still going on, with higher standards being set for the joggers, to see if they will move ahead of the hypnosis group. There is, however, one great argument on the side of hypnosis. Dr. Doney is also a heart victim. He practices self-hypnosis instead of jogging.

In the United States hypnosis has been an officially recognized method of therapy only since 1958, when the delegates to the annual meeting of the American Medical Association voted, after much cautious discussion, to approve the use of hypnosis by a doctor or by a trained hypnotist working under his direction. This vote of approval legitimatized the work of a number of American doctors who had been quietly using hypnosis for many years.

I happened to report this San Francisco convention for a documentary TV show, in the course of which I met one of these doctors, Dr. David B. Cheek, a San Francisco obstetrician-gynecologist, who has long used hypnosis both in his own practice and to assist other doctors, including surgeons who need a supplement to standard operating-room anesthesia. (This happens, for instance, with surgical patients who are also suffering from heart conditions and whose lives may be endangered by a normal dose of a chemical anesthetic.)

We got Dr. Cheek to appear on our show. Sitting around the studio waiting for show time, Cheek demonstrated to us how he uses hypnosis in helping a patient work back to some ancient, suppressed memory that may be causing him to feel symptoms induced by psychological stress. He asked the host of our show, Dr. Earl Herald (a distinguished ichthyologist, now dead) if he'd volunteer for a brief demonstration. Cheek asked Herald to sit down with his hands flat on the top of one of the studio tables. He told him he was going to hypnotize him and ask him a series of questions. If the answer was *yes,* Herald should raise the forefinger of his right hand. If the answer was *no,* he should raise the middle finger. Cheek told him that his fingers would probably lift themselves without any conscious thought.

In his scientific writings Cheek calls this technique "ideomotor responses." In conversation he calls it finger-signaling. The theory of finger-signaling, which goes back to the work of Milton H. Erickson, is that these responses tap a deeper and more reliable level of consciousness than does normal speech.

Like other experienced hypnotists, Dr. Cheek uses more than one method of inducing hypnosis. When there is time and the circumstances are favorable, he directs the subject to fix his attention on some object, which may be a plastic-ball pendulum or a flickering candle flame or a spiral disk mounted on a phonograph turntable or just a bright object, such as a wristwatch.

After the subject's eyes show signs of becoming tired, he begins an "induction talk," which may last for several minutes and which may begin like this: "Now that you are comfortable, let yourself relax as much as possible. Take a good deep breath, which helps you relax. The more you can let go, the better it will be. Keep your eyes fixed on what you are watching. Let your eyes go out of focus if you can. Take another deep breath. . . ." (The similarities to the instructions for meditation are obvious.)

On this occasion in the TV studio, as I recall, Dr. Cheek simply told Dr. Herald very firmly and very authoritatively that he was going to relax and then that he was going to go back in his imagination year by year until he had gone back to his early childhood. Cheek began to ask Herald questions about his personal life, starting in recent years and taking him back through his school years to his early childhood. Herald's fingers responded unhesitatingly until Cheek asked about something that had happened when he was about five years old. Herald suddenly shook himself, took his hands from the table, and almost angrily said, "That's gone just far enough."

(When I reminded Dr. Cheek of this incident recently, he looked troubled and said, "You know, I wonder if we'd begun to touch on something that may have been connected with Earl's heart attack.")

After the TV show Dr. Cheek went on talking about some of his experiences. The account that I remember most clearly had to do with an occasion during which Cheek was helping a surgeon and anesthesiologist with an abdominal operation.

Everything went fine until, after he'd opened the patient's abdomen, the surgeon's hand slipped and he nicked a blood vessel near the stomach. The surgeon said something like, "Oh, my god, it's filling up with blood!" Cheek suggested firmly to the patient that she drive the blood away from the vicinity of her stomach. Very shortly, he told us, the serious bleeding had stopped, and when he looked down into the abdominal cavity, the stomach had been so drained of blood that it was almost white.

This anecdote illustrates what many people think may be Cheek's most remarkable discovery—people under anesthesia are not totally unconscious but continue to hear and may respond either well or tragically to what is going on around them. When a surgeon says jovially, "Okay, gang, let's get the hell out of this hole and go home," the anesthetized patient may interpret what he hears not as a jocularity but as an announcement that the surgeon and his team are abandoning him as hopeless. At which point the patient may in fact die.

When I went back recently to find out from Dr. Cheek what had been going on during the intervening years, I found that not a great deal had changed in the medical acceptance of hypnosis. A handsome, graying man in his fifties, Cheek looked discouraged and said that he was still having a hard time getting his principal message to the surgeons. They simply didn't want to listen, but happily this was not the case with the anesthesiologists, who turned out in large numbers for the hypnosis workshops that Cheek organizes for doctors and dentists. On the whole, however, clinical hypnosis had not advanced nearly as far as he had hoped it would when the AMA first gave its blessing, back in 1958.

This is not to say that medical hypnosis has been standing still. In Portland, Oregon, Dr. Claggett Harding regularly and successfully uses hypnosis to relieve migraine. At the Massachusetts General Hospital in Boston (probably the foremost teaching hospital in the United States), Dr. Thomas P. Hackett uses hypnosis to ease the discomfort of such disagreeable procedures as passing nasograstric tubes, suturing, splinting, and changing burn dressings. He also uses hypnosis to relieve such sexual complaints as premature ejaculation and impotence. At the University of Texas Southwestern Medical Branch in Dallas, Dr. Harold B. Crasilneck uses hypnosis to help burn patients endure comfortably their otherwise tremendous pain. But most doctors continue to look on hypnosis as an unscientific and slightly disreputable proceeding.

Dr. Cheek looked considerably more cheerful when I asked about his own practice. He told me about the case of a German girl he had been called to treat after she had undergone an abortion in a Mexican border city. He found her lying on a sofa, with her legs pulled up and her hands pressing her belly. She had all the apparent symptoms of peritonitis—pain, a fever, a fast pulse, and a high respiratory rate.

Dr. Cheek found out that she was also very depressed over the abortion and was afraid her parents in Germany might find out about it. She was also worried that she might be reported to the police.

Cheek calmed her fears and told her that he wanted to give her some practice in relaxing so that the medicine he was going to give her would have a chance to work. He told her to relax every muscle in her abdomen, lettting her right index finger rise unconsciously when this had happened. A few minutes later, to the girl's great surprise, the finger trembled and lifted. Next Cheek told her to lift the finger when the pain was all gone. This time they had to wait only a little more than a minute before the finger lifted.

Within a half hour of the time he had first seen her, all tenderness was gone from the German girl's abdomen. "Her temperature was ninety-eight, pulse rate eighty-four, and respiration sixteen by the time I gave her the shot of penicillin she expected," Cheek reported. "She was back at work the next day."

In writing up this case for a scientific journal, Cheek observed, "In this case the entire picture may have been emotional, but my experience with criminal abortion cases has made me respect the role of fear, depression, and guilt in lowering resistance to pathogenic organisms within the bowel and vagina. This was the third instance of abrupt termination of fever and pain in an atmosphere of uncritical acceptance rather than punitive overtreatment."

The same basic principles can operate equally effectively with heart patients, as Cheek demonstrated recently when he appeared as a godsend to a severely distressed passenger on a plane from Omaha to Denver.

"The man I was sitting next to struck me as looking terribly green," Cheek recalled. "Not only did he seem to be in distress, but when the stewardess came around with food, he said he didn't want any. We got into conversation and I found out he was a heart patient and that he was suffering from severe angina. I also found out that he was a sales manager and that when he got to Denver he was going to have to tell one of the salesmen working for him that his territory was being cut in half. Well, he was under a good deal of stress."

Cheek suddenly looked indignant as he remembered another facet of the case. "He'd been to a heart man, who'd put him through all the tests and then had told him—if you can believe it—that 'I can't prove anything but my guess is that you'll be dead in six months.' "

Cheek snorted and went on to say that he'd then told the sales manager about a patient of his, a retired Navy man, whose heart was in such bad shape that he'd had to carry an oxygen tank around with him. He described how he'd got the sailor to work with finger signals and how they had tracked down the beginning of the trouble with his heart to something that happened early in his life. Then, Cheek had got the man to agree with him that the angina wasn't going to bother him anymore, and it hadn't.

Not surprisingly, the sales manager, who was still in great pain, was interested in this story. While their plane was put into a holding pattern over the Denver airport, he worked under Cheek's instruction with finger signals.

"I got him to regress back to his birth and found that his mother had had a hard time at the delivery," Cheek said. "He told me with his fingers that while he was being born he had felt a terrible constriction in his chest. It was obviously the source of the angina.

" 'Now,' I told him, 'you can stop punishing yourself for the hard time you caused your mother.' I got him to rehearse his angina, turning it on and turning it off. By the time we landed at Denver he had it under control. My guess is that it doesn't bother him anymore."

Unlike some other authorities on hypnosis, Cheek believes that the hypnotic state is a special state of consciousness with measurable physiological accompaniments. He regards the hypnotist as simply a convenient means for helping a person reach this state, which has deep biological roots and which occurs spontaneously with animals, with children, and with people in distress.

Cheek consequently looks on hypnosis as a completely natural thing. "It comes to our aid when we need it," he told me.

Cheek likes to nail down this point with the story of something that happened to him in Jamaica, where he had been giving a workshop in hypnosis. In the evening he went to see the show at one of the tourist hotels. A drunken guest attacked one of the native dancers with a broken beer bottle, leaving a three-inch cut in her scalp. Both the girl and the audience went into a brief spontaneous trance state that was not broken until, looking down, the girl saw blood on her arm and dress. It was not her own blood, for she had hardly bled at all, but her assailant's.

Cheek reached her side just as her trance turned into frightened alertness and blood began to gush from the cut. He put his thumb on her forehead just above her nose and said loudly and authoritatively, "Listen to me. You are all right. Stop that bleeding!"

The dancer's face went back to the trance state and within two minutes the rush of blood had become a slight ooze. The wound did not bleed when Cheek examined it with his finger to see if there were particles of glass in it or if there was a depressed fracture. Nor did the wound bleed during the hour before a local doctor arrived to sew it up.

In a technical account of the case Dr. Cheek wrote, "We do not know whether this stopping of hemorrhage is brought about through changes in force fields, changes in muscle tone, or inhibition of the transfer of precurosers to active fibrinolysins in the injured area."

But he said to me, "When people are really in trouble, they go into hypnosis."

## HYPNOSIS AND PAIN

"We'd be simply overwhelmed if we opened the doors to people who need help, particularly if they're in pain," Dr. Ernest R. Hilgard told me when I visited him at the hypnosis laboratory he founded at Stanford.

Hilgard went on to tell me about the case of a young woman who had come to his laboratory suffering from excruciating pain after an automobile accident. Hilgard and his associates not only relieved her pain but taught her to use hypnosis to cope with her other problems, which included a tendency to overweight and sleeplessness. Reminded of a recent visit from his patient, Hilgard laughed and said, "When I saw her last week, she said her husband gets so mad at her now because whenever she wants to sleep, she can just close her eyes and get to sleep like *that*."

Dr. Hilgard does not match anybody's preconception of what a hypnotist should look like. Nearing seventy, he is a grave and serious man with a quick and rather shy smile. A graduate of the University of Illinois with a PhD from Yale, he is the most academically eminent American researcher into the nature of hypnosis.

An interest in finding ways to study such phenomena as represssion and dreams led Hilgard toward hypnosis. As he recalls the founding of his laboratory, "When Stanford got thirty million dollars from the Ford Foundation for health studies, I got a little of that Ford money to start the hypnosis lab."

Located on the second floor of Jordan Hall, one of the ancient sandstone buildings that make up Stanford's Old Quad, the hypnosis lab occupies remodeled quarters consisting of a suite of offices and four small laboratories, each equipped with a chair and with instruments that record the bodily functions of the subject.

"Interestingly enough, hypnosis doesn't turn out to be terribly remote from my earlier work," Hilgard told me. "I've always been interested in problems of voluntary and involuntary control. In psychology we tend to study animals, their psychology and sensory processes, but these problems don't have very much to do with the really deep problems of our times. In hypnosis research you're right up against the problems of consciousness and unconsciousness, of social influence, of control of mind over body, of psychosomatic problems."

Currently Hilgard is engaged in a lively argument going on among some scientists over what hypnosis really is. His opponents prefer always to use quotation marks around the word. They do not deny, however, that hypnosis (or "hypnosis") really works. Reputable observers, both scientists and laymen, have reported a wide variety of effects. In the field of clinical applications alone, hypnosis, as we have seen, has served not only as a nonchemical anesthetic and a substitute for jogging but has also been used to mitigate the pangs of withdrawal from narcotics, to improve myopia, to alleviate ichthyosis ("fish-skin disease"), and to ease chronic unendurable pain.

Pain represents the extreme of physical stress that afflicts human beings. With the exception of a small number of people born without the capacity to feel pain, pain is a universal experience, and its alleviation is one of the primary tasks of the physician—second only to the preservation of life itself.

The intensity of pain and its disabling effect as a stressor ranges from such a minor pain as that of a hypodermic needle puncturing the skin to such unendurable and intractable pains as are associated with massive burns, some forms of cancer, and the tic douloureux, or neuralgia of the trigeminal nerve. Whoever can provide a means of easing such pain without the use of narcotics or the surgical severance of nerves will be remembered as a great benefactor of mankind.

As Dr. Hilgard pointed out to me, the phenomenon of pain confronts us with a number of still unsolved puzzles. To begin with, we are not always sure where a pain actually is. Consider the common case of heartburn, a digestive disorder whose pain is felt in the chest rather than the abdomen. Or consider the heart victim who commonly reports an intense pain in his left arm. Or consider the case of cancer patients who have had their spinal cords cut to relieve their pain. When the deadened lower parts of their bodies are pricked, they sometimes report pain in their chests or backs.

A related part of the puzzle has to do with the common observation that individuals react to pain with a variety of responses. A pain that puts one person out of action is only a

minor annoyance to another. When we attempt to relieve
disabling pain with drugs, the results are not always what we
expect. Hilgard told me of an experiment into the relief of
pain after surgery. When postsurgical patients were given
both morphine and a placebo, one-third of them reported
they got as much relief from the placebo as from the morphine. Another third were relieved neither by the morphine
nor by the placebo. Only a third were relieved more by the
morphine than by the placebo. Which group was the "normal" group?

At the Stanford lab, work has been done in such clinical
fields as controlling the pain of migraine headache and terminal cancer through hypnosis, but the most solidly scientific
work has had to do with the control of artificially created
pain.

In Hilgard's experiments controllable pain is produced in
laboratory subjects through two methods. In one, the flow of
blood into the arm is cut off by a tourniquet. In the other, the
subject's hand is immersed in circulating ice water. Both
methods produce severe pain.

Hilgard's subjects are students—Stanford students during
the school year and local high school youngsters during
summer vacation. Some of these youngsters showed marked
hypnotic abilities, and the experiments in which they took
part demonstrated that some people can learn easily to control pain.

In understanding the hypnotic control of pain, Hilgard
told me, two factors had to be kept in mind. The first was
that pain cannot be controlled simply through relaxation,
even the profound relaxation that can be produced by hypnosis. Experimental subjects with their hands in ice water
would feel pain until the positive suggestion was made that
pain wouldn't be felt. After this, the subject would cheerfully
leave his arm in the ice water as long as the experimenter
wanted.

The second factor, Hilgard emphasized, was that this removal of pain was not just a hallucination. As the laboratory

measurements showed, the bodies of the subjects reacted exactly as if no pain were in fact present.

"As a person is put under pain," Hilgard explained, "the blood pressure normally rises, giving you a physiological indicator showing that the pain is really working. But when we reduce the pain by hypnosis, you just don't get that rise in blood pressure. This gives us evidence that we're really getting control."

The high school and college youngsters outdid their instructors in the ingenuity of the methods they used to abolish pain, and thereby underlined the importance of the imagination in successful hypnosis. The hypnotist stroked their arms and told them their arms would become numb as if they had been anesthetized. It turned out that most of the subjects had simply ignored these suggestions and done it their own way.

One young man of a musical bent imagined during the experiment that he was singing a duet with a friend; he was so carried away that he expressed irritation when, every five minutes, the experimenter asked for a pain report. Others imagined they had switches in their brains, which they pretended to turn off.

The most ingenious of all was a young woman who had visited the Louvre during a vacation trip to Europe. With her hand in freezing cold water, she imagined that she was inside Venus de Milo without any arm to hurt. It worked fine except that, Hilgard says, she reported a slight tingling in one shoulder.

## THE NATURAL HISTORY OF HYPNOSIS

Arguments about the medical respectability of hypnosis have been going on ever since Franz Anton Mesmer, an eighteenth-century Austrian physician excited the *haut monde* of Vienna and Paris by his demonstrations of "animal magnetism," which later came to be called "mesmerism."

Mesmer's most celebrated case was that of Maria Paradis, a musician who suffered from what in later years would have been called hysterical blindness. Mesmer took the lady into his house and cured her. When her parents, fearful that Maria might lose her government pension, forced her to leave Mesmer's household, she went blind again. Encouraged to leave Vienna by the hostility of the orthodox medical community, Mesmer left for Paris, where animal magnetism again became a topic of fashionable conversation.

Mesmer's career in Paris was brought to an end when, in 1784, a royal commission, whose members included Benjamin Franklin, filed a negative report on his medical activities. Although recognizing the remarkable cures Mesmer had brought about, the commission condemned animal magnetism as a principle of therapy and proposed instead that the cures had been effected by some as-yet-unknown physiological process.

As a result of the commission's hostility, poor Mesmer lost his practice and retired to Versailles. He died in obscurity in Switzerland.

The nineteenth century was the golden age of medical hypnosis. The first tooth was extracted under hypnosis in 1823. In 1826 a woman gave birth painlessly under hypnosis. In the 1840's James Esdaile, a British surgeon working in a prison hospital in India, used hypnosis as his only anesthetic in more than 3,000 operations, of which 300 were major surgery, including amputations.

Esdaile noted a remarkable phenomenon besides the reduction or absence of pain: His mortality rate from postoperative infection dropped from 50 percent to 5 percent. This phenomenon has been noted frequently. As Dr. Cheek explains it, the subconscious mind under hypnotic anesthesia enables the body to develop greater resistance to infection.

After returning to England from his successful career in India, Esdaile, in the highest tradition of organized medicine, was put on trial by the British Medical Association. He was found guilty and lost his license.

Esdaile was not the only well-known British doctor to be destroyed professionally by his interest in hypnosis. John

Elliotson, who had introduced the stethoscope to England and who was appointed to the first chair of medicine at London University, was drummed out of his profession in 1838 because he conducted public exhibitions of mesmerism. He later founded an institution he called a "mesmeric hospital."

The word "hypnotism" was coined in 1842 by the Scottish surgeon James Braid, one of the pioneer investigators of the phenonemon. ("Hypnosis" is nowadays preferred by scientific workers in the field, but it is a newer coinage.) Braid originally used the term "neurohypnotism" to describe the "state or condition of nervous sleep," but a year later he dropped the prefix and after that "hypnotism" stood on its own—except when it was called "mesmerism" or "Braidism."

In spite of demonstrations by Esdaile and others that hypnosis was effective as a surgical anesthetic, it was never widely used. A powerful factor in its decline was the discovery of chemical anesthetics, such as ether and chloroform.

The dramatic introduction of ether into the operating room was made in 1846, when the first proponent of ether, the Boston dentist William T. G. Morton, served as anesthetist at the Massachusetts General Hospital while Dr. J. C. Warren painlessly removed a neck tumor from an unconscious patient. At the end of the operation Dr. Warren turned to the skeptical audience and declared, "Gentlemen, this is no humbug." One can only speculate on the consequences if the operation had been performed under hypnosis instead.

Interest in the medical uses of hypnosis continued throughout the century, though in a somewhat subdued form. In France a country doctor, A. A. Liébeault, ministered to villagers with treatments based on hypnosis and acquired wide attention. Liébeault reinforced the powers of suggestion by declining to accept a fee for a hypnotic cure, while charging the regular fee when he administered a drug.

In the latter years of the nineteenth century hypnosis was picked up by the pioneers of the growing professions of neurology and psychiatry. The great Jean Martin Charcot became interested and experimented with hypnosis at the Salpêtrière, his clinic in Paris. The even greater Sigmund Freud picked up his teacher Charcot's interest. When, with his colleague Josef Breuer, Freud published his epochal *Studies in Hysteria* in 1895, hypnosis was the method of treatment they described.

In 1899 Freud wrote that he had seen "old Liébeault working among the poor women and children of the laboring classes; I was a spectator of [Hippolyte] Bernheim's astonishing experiments upon his hospital patients; and I received the profoundest impression of the possibility that there could be powerful mental processes which nevertheless remained hidden from the consciousness of men."

Five years later, however, Freud publicly abandoned hypnosis because, as he wrote, "it conceals the resistance and for this reason obstructs the physician's insight into the play of the psychic forces."

Freud added a provocative footnote the next year in his *Three Essays on the Theory of Sexuality*, in which he suggested that the relation between the hypnotist and his subject is an unconsciously sexual one, with the subject masochistically making himself amenable to the hypnotist's will. Supporters of hypnosis have argued that Freud's real trouble with hypnosis was that he was a poor hypnotist. Whatever the reasons, Freud's abandonment marked the beginning of another period of neglect.

Although some psychiatrists, dentists, psychologists and anesthesiologists continued to use hypnosis, its medical usage was largely in eclipse for about half a century. Hilgard has explained its revival as owing in some measure to the social unrest of the past twenty years that has seen the growth of the drug culture and of a revived interest in mysticism, meditative practices, and the problems of human growth.

The new era was officially opened by the 1958 resolution of the AMA to permit doctors to use hypnosis. A similar resolution had been passed by the British Medical Association three years earlier.

## WHAT IS HYPNOSIS?

Ernest Hilgard is the most prominent scientific champion of the classic notion of hypnosis as a special trance state induced by the hypnotist, or, after training, by the subject himself. (The innocent idea that the trance is induced by the compelling power of the hypnotist's eyes is neatly shot down by the professional career of Dr. William Chapman, a psychiatrist at the University of Virginia hospital in Charlottesville, who uses hypnosis in his practice. Dr. Chapman is blind.)

Hilgard's principal opponent in the scholarly journals that devote attention to hypnosis is Dr. Theodore Xenophon Barber, who maintains that the trance is unnecessary and "unparsimonious," since all the effects that can be produced in the trance state can be produced without a trance.

Although the two men are at swords' points professionally, they are friendly outside the jousting halls of the journals. With his wry smile Hilgard described to me the last occasion on which Barber had visited his Stanford lab, which was set up for the ice-water experiments.

"Barber just wasn't troubled by the pain at all although everybody else found it excruciating," Hilgard said. And he added with a trace of envy, "He was brought up in Greece, where he walked on coals as a little boy."

When I asked Barber about these experiences, he told me that while he was a boy, he had lived in Greece for a while and, with the other children of the village, had, on ceremonial occasions, followed the adults across a pit full of burning charcoal. He went on to say, "The pit was set up in such a way that if you walked across quickly, you simply did not burn. Those who were nervous and tarried usually did get blisters."

Barber objected strenuously, however, to the suggestion that this had anything to do with his ability to hypnotize himself. When he began working with hypnosis, he told me, he wasn't a responsive subject, "because I didn't think that I

was the kind of person who was 'suggestible' or 'hypnotiza-
ble' and I did not believe that I could experience the suggested effects." After he allowed his thinking and imagining
to move with the suggestions, he found that he could have
hypnotic experiences—or as he prefers to write it, "hypnotic"
experiences.

Hardheaded people have always tended to dismiss hypnosis as quackery. Some of Barber's public pronouncements
have offered aid and comfort to these critics, for he has
stripped away much of the mystery from the phenomenon.
It is easy for a careless jumper to leap to the conclusion that
there is no such thing as hypnosis, or, as *Time* magazine once
announced, hypnosis is nothing but a put-on. But this is not
at all what Barber is saying.

The bones of Barber's argument is that the trance is not
necessary. A trance (or a state of deep relaxation) can indeed
be produced as one of the effects of hypnosis, but all the
effects that can be produced with a trance can also be produced without a trance.

"What I mean by hypnosis is very simple," Barber told me
as we sat in his small, book-lined, institutional-green office in
the research building of the state hospital at Medfield, Massachusetts. "You tell a person to relax, and then you give
suggestions. Operationally or concretely that's what it is. You
may give suggestions that you're going into a deep, deep
hypnotic state, or you may not."

If the hypnotic state didn't depend on a trance, I asked
Barber, what did it depend on?

"What they call hypnosis is really a series of suggestions,"
he told me. "How you respond to these suggestions depends
on a lot of things. In other words, you'll respond to the
suggestions if you're *set* to do so and if you take a cooperative
attitude and if you let yourself think along with them. That's
what they really mean by hypnosis. It's quite different from
saying that there's something different, and special, and mysterious about it. And that's why I put the word *hypnosis* in
quotation marks."

As Barber has pointed out, his theory of hypnosis is not novel. As long ago as 1924, H. R. Wells, working with male college students, obtained the usual hypnotic effects without putting his subjects into a hypnotic trance. Wells reported that direct commands, repeated emphatically, worked as well as hypnotic induction for producing anesthesia, amnesia, limb rigidity, hallucinatory pain, total amnesia, and various types of posthypnotic behavior.

I asked how stage hypnosis worked. Barber, who is a dark, beaky, spectacled man in his middle forties, laughed and got up to look for a match. When he found one, he said, "Look. Here's one of the things they do on stage to a 'hypnotized' subject."

He lighted the match and held it under the palm of his right hand, which was facing downward. With the flame touching the skin of his palm, he moved the match slowly from the base of his hand to the end of his fingers and back. Then he blew out the flame and turned his hand over. There were carbon smudges on his skin but no blisters or other signs of burning.

"That's all there is to it," Barber said. "As long as you keep the flame moving, you'll never burn yourself and it doesn't matter at all if you're hypnotized or not."

(The match trick creates a powerful illusion. When I tried it myself later, I felt only a moderate discomfort from the heat, but the lady I was with shuddered, gasped, and asked me not to do anything like that again.)

Barber qualifies as an expert on stage hypnosis because he once enrolled in a school for stage hypnotists. It was an interesting experience. Barber found that the extraordinary performances an accomplished hypnotist can produce depend largely on the selection of naturally suggestible volunteers whose willingness to cooperate is reinforced by the dramatic setting and most particularly by the expectations of the audience.

The stage hypnotist takes no chances. While he appears to be putting his subject in a trance, he may actually be whispering an invitation for the subject to cooperate with him in fooling the audience. (The *Encyclopedia of Stage Hypnotism* suggests: "We are going to have some good laughs on the audience and fool them . . . so when I tell you to do some funny things, do exactly as I secretly tell you. OK? Swell!")

Hypnotists will take advantage of a lack of outright challenge as evidence of success. In a common demonstration the subject is told to hold one of his arms outright. Both the subject and the audience are told that the outstretched arm is stiff and unbendable. But the hypnotist doesn't actually ask the subject to try to bend his arm. The subject goes along because he doesn't want to embarrass the hypnotist or the expectant audience. And, for all he knows, maybe he *can't* bend his arm.

Some of the most dramatic effects are obtained by trickery or the knowledge of physiological facts that have nothing to do with hypnosis. The "human plank" feat, for example, is easily reproducible by an unhypnotized person, simply because the human body when supported horizontally by a chair under the feet and a chair under the head is surprisingly strong and rigid. (Anybody who tries this experiment should be sure, if he is going to support another person's weight, that the chair supports his shoulders as well.)

Outright trickery is resorted to in the demonstration in which the hypnotist causes the subject's pulse to disappear. The most common way to make sure that the blood flow is cut off is to tape a golf ball into the armpit of a confederate. When the stooge presses down on the ball, an artery is compressed and the blood flow cut off.

Barber's description of the stage hypnotist's methods is supported by the poet and essayist L. E. Sissman's diverting account in the *Atlantic Monthly* of his own youthful experience as a volunteer subject for an itinerant hypnotist.

Sissman recalled, "After about five minutes of this trance-inducing behavior on his part, I came to the sudden realization that, for reasons traceable either to his technique or my immalleability, nothing was happening; quite clearly, it was

just not going to take. This was followed with a rising desire
to laugh uproariously at the whole farcial proceeding,
thwarted by an even stronger order from my superego to
play the good subject and see the damned thing through.
Just as I had resolved upon this course—I felt his *honor* was at
stake and must be vindicated—he nearly blew the gaff (and
my resolve) by telling me, 'You are now in a psychotic state.'
Converting an involuntary snort into a deep-sleeper's sigh, I
soldiered on."

Sissman's experience is precisely in line with Barber's observation that the stage hypnotist is really an actor playing,
badly or well, the part of a hypnotist. And it works. Sissman
did not leave the stage but soldiered on to avoid embarrassing the hypnotist in front of his audience.

Barber and others, such as T. R. Sarbin of the University
of California at Santa Cruz, have looked at laboratory hypnosis with the same skeptical gaze they have directed at stage
hypnosis. Like Barber, Sarbin maintains that hypnosis is
essentially role playing, with the subject adopting the role
assigned to him by the hypnotist and then playing this role
out as well as he can. This hard-nosed attitude has not en-
deared these scientists to their colleagues. Hilgard, for one,
rather testily describes Barber and Sarbin as "enemies from
within . . . who make a special point of holding a skeptical,
debunking attitude."

If hypnosis is nothing but suggestibility and role playing,
what is left?

A good deal, apparently. I must fall back on my personal
experience, for in the end what happens to each of us is the
most convincing demonstration of what is true. Whatever
hypnosis is, it works—and it works most particularly in helping the process of letting go.

Almost twenty years ago I went out to San Quentin prison
as a teacher in order to keep my family fed and clothed while
I worked on a novel. I was also doing other things, such as
working as *Newsweek*'s stringer in San Francisco. The point is
that although I was young and healthy I was also regularly

pushing myself pretty hard—and I was feeling the stress.

On the night with which this account is concerned, I'd come home at dinnertime feeling as if I'd been stretched on a rack. I'd interviewed somebody for *Newsweek* in the morning, filed a brief story from the Western Union office at noon, and taught at the prison all afternoon. Not only was I mentally exhausted and irritable, but my bones ached. I was done in. I had a drink, which didn't do me much good, and then sat down to dinner, grumbling at the kids, who felt perfectly fine and were full of childish chatter.

In the midst of dinner the phone rang. It was the principal of the San Quentin school, asking if I'd mind coming back within the hour to substitute for a night-school teacher who'd just called in sick. I said I'd mind very much, that I was absolutely dead and I'd be damned if I'd fill in for somebody who was probably malingering anyway.

The principal, who was in fact a good fellow, persisted. It wouldn't, he said, take very much out of me because it was a public-speaking class. Friday nights were devoted to an open forum during which any man in the class could get up and talk for five minutes on any subject he wanted to except sex and crime. All I'd have to do was to monitor the speeches and see that the discussion didn't slop over into the forbidden areas. Finally I said I'd do it (I'm a good fellow too), finished my dinner in a hurry, and drove over to the prison, feeling perfectly terrible and more than a little sorry for myself.

The public-speaking class turned out to be a milestone event. There was no particular reason it should be. As the principal had promised me, it was easy duty. One of the prisoners would ask to speak, come up to the rostrum, and we'd listen critically to him. Some of the talks were good, and some weren't. I felt dull, tired, and my bones still ached.

Then a prisoner I shall call Devane got up. He was a large, good-looking, young black man with a preacher's rich voice. As I recall, Devane was doing time for murder in the second degree.

"I'd like to say a few words about hypnosis," he said. He went on to tell us that he'd learned the technique from a psychiatrist at Mendocino State Hospital, where the criminally insane were incarcerated. Since hypnosis didn't have anything to do with either sex or crime, I told him to go ahead.

"Gentlemen," Devane said, "I'm going to ask you to take part in a simple test for suggestibility. Please clasp your hands. Like this." He demonstrated by putting his hands together with the fingers interlaced. I followed his instructions, as did most of the class. "Now I want you to clasp your hands together tighter and tighter and tighter, just as tightly as you can."

Devane held up his own hands and showed us his straining knuckles. He said, "You are squeezing your hands so tightly together that you're not going to be able to pull them apart. Even when I ask you to pull them apart, you'll find they don't want to come. Your hands are going to cling to each other as tightly as if they were glued together."

He looked around the classroom, where almost everybody was sitting with his hands clasped in his lap, face raised expectantly. We looked rather like a meeting of a quietist religious sect. "Now try to pull your hands apart," Devane said.

My hands came apart without any trouble. I felt cheated, but as I looked around the classroom, I saw that several men were still tugging at their locked knuckles while others were staring at the palms of their hands as if they expected to find them covered with glue.

Devane looked pleased. "Anybody who had trouble pulling his hands apart is probably a good subject for hypnosis," he said. "Now I'd like to go one step further."

After some discussion—there was one fellow in the class who thought this whole business was out of order—we voted to let Devane go ahead.

"Gentlemen, I want you to relax," he said. "Sit back in your chairs and let your muscles unwind themselves. Let your head flop back or let it flop forward or anything you find comfortable and try to think of nothing at all."

The men adopted a variety of relaxed attitudes while Devane continued to talk. I guessed that his patter must have been pretty close to the professional hypnotist's patter. It went like this: "You feel completely relaxed and you want to fall asleep . . . Your eyelids are becoming heavy . . . heavy . . . heavy. . . . You want to close them and go to sleep. . . . You want to rest. . . . You are tired and sleepy and your eyelids are heavy . . . oh so heavy. . . . It's going to feel so good to rest . . . so good to rest . . . just to sleep for a few minutes and then to wake up and find the tiredness is all gone."

I felt comfortable and relaxed, but I remember that as I watched Devane through half-closed eyes, I felt disappointed that I hadn't gone into the classic hypnotic trance. As it turned out, something profound *had* been happening to me, for when Devane was through and I got up to take the rostrum myself, I must have stood there for a full half-minute without saying anything.

The reason I was silent was that I was in the process of finding out that I simply wasn't tired anymore. Although the demonstration had taken no more than five or six minutes, I felt as if I'd just woken up from a particularly satisfying and refreshing night-long sleep. The aches in my bones were gone as if they'd never been there. My muscles were springy. My mind was clear and fresh, and I would willingly have taken on a new day's work. I felt absolutely great.

Several years later, after I'd met Dr. Cheek, I told him about my experience at San Quentin. "Why, of course," he said, as if it were the most natural thing in the world.

And so in the end it need make no difference to us if Hilgard is right or if Barber is right, if hypnosis is an altered state of awareness or if it is nothing but suggestibility and role playing. The fact of the matter simply is that as a means of letting go, hypnosis works.

## ACUPUNCTURE AND HYPNOANESTHESIA

Whether or not acupuncture can best be explained as a medical application of hypnosis is a question we cannot answer at the present time. On the balance of the evidence it seems likely that it contains a large component of hypnosis. Furthermore, acupuncture carries with it important implications for achieving internal and external harmony and letting go.

Our ignorance of the true nature of acupuncture is not due to any lack of attention. Since 1971, when James Reston of the New York *Times* underwent his well-reported appendectomy under acupuncture anesthesia, a seemingly unending parade of Western physicians has marched through Chinese hospitals and then come home to report on what they have seen.

There is no question that they have seen something remarkable—remarkable at least to us Westerners with our prejudices in favor of inducing anesthesia by introducing poisonous substances into our bodies. The message of these observers is clear: Whatever acupuncture is, it works.

Typical of the eyewitness accounts was that of Dr. P. E. Brown, a British medical man who, at the operating room of a Shanghai hospital, saw a young man in his thirties lose part of his lung under acupuncture anesthesia alone.

"He was fully conscious and able to speak to me," Dr. Brown reported. "There was only one acupuncture point, situated over the right biceps. A needle two inches long was inserted and manually rotated by the 'anesthetist.' She was rapidly rotating the needle for ten to fifteen seconds, at intervals of half a minute."

The patient conversed calmly with Brown, who noted that his pulse and blood pressure were normal. He insisted he felt no pain.

Reports such as this aroused a lively interest in the United States, which had been the Western country probably most ignorant of its uses. (In France a Westernized version of acupuncture had been in use for many years.)

Public demonstrations were held, some of them sponsored by medical societies. Acupuncturists, some of them experienced and some of them ninety-day-wonders, hung out their shingles. Laws were passed regulating acupuncture and acupuncturists, and the newspapers carried regular reports of the successes and failures of acupuncture as an anesthetic and as a technique of healing such disabling illnesses as rheumatoid arthritis.

By the summer of 1973 scientists at twenty-six medical schools as well as at independent research institutes were exploring acupuncture. One of the most active research programs was at the White Memorial Medical Center in Los Angeles.

At White fifteen major operations had been done under acupuncture as the anesthetic. Among the operations were a breast biopsy, the amputation of a leg, and the removal of a gallbladder.

The patients were each given a shot of morphine before the operations, but as the anesthesiologist at one of these operations remarked to a skeptic, "I think if we gave you that small amount of morphine and operated on you without the acupuncture, you'd scream your head off."

Other clinical reports have given varying verdicts on the usefulness of acupuncture. Not all American investigators are convinced that it has any value at all. The head of the department of anesthesiology at the University of California medical school in San Francisco, Dr. William K. Hamilton, has remained vocally unbelieving. He has declared that acupuncture in dentistry is almost totally useless while attempts to use acupuncture to ease the pains of childbirth have shown "underwhelming" results. Other faculty members at UCSF have compared belief in acupuncture with belief in the shrine at Lourdes or with Christian Science —comparisons that may in fact be two-edged swords. It does appear that belief has a good deal to do with acupuncture's successes.

With their usual good sense the Chinese maintain that

acupuncture works because it promotes harmony between yin and yang, a theory that has served them well for many hundreds of years. In view of our chronic reluctance to learn from less "scientific" societies, it is both surprising and refreshing to discover that yin and yang have not been totally ignored by our medical scientists.

Two medical-school professors at Los Angeles, Dr. Gerald Looney of the USC medical school and Dr. Richard Kroening, a rheumatologist at UCLA, have recently put forward the yet-to-be-proved argument that acupuncture is a precise method for promoting balance between the sympathetic and parasympathetic branches of the nervous system.

Looney and Kroening argue that stress disorders are brought on by imbalance in the autonomic nervous system. The traditional 365 acupuncture points, they believe, are precisely located for the stimulation of either the sympathetic division or the parasympathetic division, thus bringing the system into balance. One can be pardoned for suspecting that old Ch'i Po, the Yellow Emperor's doctor, knew this all the time.

A more characteristically Western explanation of acupuncture that has received wide acceptance is that proposed by Dr. Ronald Melzack, a psychologist at McGill University in Montreal. Rejecting the yin-yang theory because it is too unscientific, Melzack formulated what he calls the "gate control" theory, which both explains some of the puzzles of pain and provides an explanation for the effectiveness of acupuncture.

Briefly the gate-control theory suggests that something like a gate exists in the pain-signaling system. If the gate is open, signals from injured tissue can make their way to the brain. If the gate is closed, the pain is never felt. According to Melzack, large fibers in the sensory nerves that run from the skin to the central nervous system tend to "close the gate" when they are stimulated; small fibers in the same nerves tend to "open the gate." The acupuncture needle stimulates the large fibers, closes the gate, and stops the transmission of pain.

Melzack recognizes cultural training and suggestion as important additives in acupuncture, but he specifically rejects hypnosis as an ingredient.

Theodore Barber gives a greater emphasis to suggestion than does Melzack and bases his explanation of acupuncture on a less complex physiological explanation.

Barber points out that our notions about the sensitivity of the body to pain are usually somewhat overstated—we simply are less sensitive than we think. In support of his position he cites research work that has shown that the brain, compact bone, the lungs, the surface of the heart, the liver, the spleen, the kidney, the stomach, the jejunum, the ileum, the colon, and the uterus can be cut without pain.

"What happens," Barber told me, "is that you cut through the skin. That hurts, but even so it's fairly quick. The deeper you go, the more insensitive the internal organs are. The skin continues to hurt, but it's not that intolerably painful, particularly if you're relaxed and not all that anxious. We overemphasize the pain of surgery tremendously. Before 1840 everybody underwent surgery without drugs, and some people *were* able to tolerate it—maybe ten percent."

This natural tolerance to pain, Barber pointed out, has been more encouraged in the Chinses culture than in ours. Furthermore, the patient's anxiety is relieved by tranquilizers and analgesics. Finally the acupuncture needles themselves distract the patient from the pain that is left.

Barber's view of the matter is supported by the reports of medical men who have used drugless anesthesia. As long ago as 1956, at the Chicago Lying-In Hospital, Drs. S. T. Lee and William S. Kroger first performed a hysterectomy entirely under hypnoanesthesia. Since then, Kroger, who now practices in Beverly Hills, has performed many other surgical procedures, major and minor, without drugs of any sort.

Dr. Kroger recently commented on acupuncture in these

words: "My explanation for acupunctural analgesia is that the Chinese have rediscovered the effectiveness of preconditioning, autogenic training, yoga breathing exercises, and a form of 'suggestion in slow motion—hypnosis.' These methods allay the fear and apprehension of selected patients and raise the pain threshold. In the environment in which acupunctural analgesia is used, it is obviously the method of choice."

Surgery without anesthetics is also found in Eastern Europe. Sheila Ostrander and Lynn Shroeder reported on a Bulgarian drugless surgeon, Georgi Lazanov, who, as Esdaile did in the last century, found that drugless surgery speeds healing of the incision and reduces the danger of infection. Lozanov calls his method "thought anesthesia."

In sum acupuncture and drugless surgery appear to depend in a great measure on the patient's cultural conditioning and on his belief that he won't feel pain. This observation is borne out by the experience of people who have discovered that they can cope with pain without the help of a hypnotist or an acupuncturist.

One of these fortunate people is Barber himself. When I asked him how he coped with pain in Hilgard's laboratory situations, Barber told me, "I don't think of stimulation as pain. Instead I continue to think of the hand and fingers as a rubbery lump of matter 'out there.' "

Barber manages his visits to the dentist in much the same way, thinking of the drilling and other dental experiences simply as sensations that are rather interesting in themselves. He reports that he feels no anxiety, distress, or pain.

I once heard Jack Schwartz, a faith healer who has replicated at a lab at the Menninger Clinic the feats of Indian fakirs—he pushes knitting needles through his arms—explain to an audience how he does this without pain. Schwartz, who speaks with a powerful Dutch accent, said, "If you would take the needle and you would sneak behind me and you put it in my buttocks or anywhere else, I would jump up too and scream out, but if you told me you were going to do that, then I would know that I had to be alert to control it so no pain is felt. I detach myself from this physical body and from the outside, indeed, get the image that the blood will keep flowing and that in a way you make it flow so fast that it hardly can even get out of your vein."

A remarkable feature of Schwartz's performance is that he not only appears to feel no pain but that he also loses practically no blood from the puncture wounds. He claims that he has never been infected, even after deliberately making his needles dirty.

Some months after hearing Schwartz, I managed to develop a rather painful swelling between the nail and the first knuckle of my right index finger. The swelling didn't hurt enough to send me straightaway to a doctor, but it throbbed and was a disagreeable nuisance, particularly since I was traveling at the time.

Remembering the experiences of Hilgard's students and the advice of Barber and Schwartz, I decided to try to get rid of the pain. I imagined that my finger was a lump of clay out there and that there was a switch in my shoulder that could turn off the pain. After a little practice in this imaginative exercise, I found to my grateful surprise that whenever the throbbing pain made itself felt, I could simply turn it off.

This experience was fresh in my mind when I arrived at Dr. Margolin's laboratory at the University of Colorado medical center. Something Margolin said reminded me of my success, and I told him my story.

Margolin nodded and answered, "I'm not surprised. When you learned you could influence this, you found a way to trigger your right to ignore it."

Asserting one's right to ignore something that hurts is a powerful device in coping with the stress of pain.


## AUTOGENIC TRAINING

I was introduced to autogenic training by Elmer and Alyce [pronounced A-lees] Green at the same seminar in San Francisco at which I heard Jack Schwartz talk. The Greens, who had been working on autogenic training at their laboratory at the Menninger Foundation since 1967, reported on their recent findings and called up a volunteer for a demonstration.

Mrs. Green, a pleasant-faced, gray-haired woman, told the volunteer that she was going to put him through an autogenic session very much like that experienced by the volunteers in the laboratory. His part in the demonstration would be to relax as completely as he could while he listened to her repeat instructions that are known as autogenic phrases.

Elmer Green taped a thermistor—a delicate electrical device that measures changes in temperature—to the palm of the volunteer's hand. The volunteer's success in relaxing would be measured by whether or not he managed to raise the temperature of his hands. Elmer Green sat down opposite him to monitor the meter.

Mrs. Green suggested that the rest of us make ourselves as comfortable as we could, close our eyes, and follow the instructions she would be giving the volunteer. She told us she would be giving us three sets of autogenic phrases. (*Autogenic* means self-generated.)

The first set of phrases would be directed toward relaxing the striped muscles of our bodies—the muscles we use when we move our arms and legs. The second set of phrases would tend to warm the hands and relax the smooth muscles of the body such as those that control the diameter of the blood vessels. The third set of exercises would quiet our minds. She said she would pause after each phrase to give us time to repeat the phrase to ourselves.

The first set started like this:
*"I feel quite quiet.*
*"I am beginning to feel quite relaxed,*
*"My feet feel heavy and relaxed,"* and went on.
The second set started like this:
*"I am quite relaxed,*
*"My arms and my hands are heavy and warm,*
*"I feel quite quiet,"* and went on.

The third set started,
*"My whole body is quiet, comfortable, relaxed,*
*"My mind is quiet,"* and ended, after some more phrases,
*"I feel an inward quietness."*

Mrs. Green told us to repeat such thoughts silently for several minutes.

When the few minutes were up, Mrs. Green said, "All right, that concludes the relaxation and reverie, and I'd like you to reactivate the body now by taking a deep breath and thinking the following phrases: 'I feel life and energy flowing back through my legs, hips, solar plexus, chest, arms and hands, neck and head. The energy makes me feel light and alive.' " She finished by telling us to take deep breaths and stretch.

Elmer Green, who is a cheerful, spectacled man with an old-fashioned crew cut, asked the volunteer to describe his sensations during the session.

The volunteer, a middle-aged man, said that he had felt a great sense of peace and harmony. "The body seemed to be very much relaxed," he told us. "I felt very comfortable and at ease. Further, I had thought I had felt nervous prior to coming up, nervous or excited, one of the two. Then, as I went through the training, I felt very calm, very peaceful."

Dr. Green was pleased with this report, but he said he had contradictory information from the meter he had been monitoring. Instead of becoming warmer as he repeated the autogenic phrases, the volunteer's hands had become colder. As Green reported this, I realized that my own hands were clammy and cold.

"Well," Green said briskly, "your response was just about what we get with half of the people who do it. With half of the people it gets cool, and with half it gets a little bit warmer." He explained that it probably had something to do with our conditioning to stress situations, and he predicted that with further training our hands would indeed get warm.

And, in fact, that was the way it turned out for me.

Autogenic training is an ambitious application of the principles of hypnosis to the problems of stress and stress-related disease. It is much better known in Europe and Japan than it is in the United States.

Autogenic training was invented in the 1890's by a Berlin brain physiologist named Oskar Vogt, who observed that patients could be easily taught to hypnotize themselves through a system he devised of simple mental exercises. The patients reported that they felt heavy and warm as their tiredness and tension disappeared. Their headaches went away and they seemed to find it easier to cope with their daily problems. Vogt gave his discovery the truly Germanic title *Prophylaktische Ruhe-Autohypnosen,* or "prophylactic rest-autohypnosis."

A younger Berlin psychiatrist, Johannes H. Schultz, took up Vogt's work in 1905, following up his own interest in the clinical applications of hypnosis. (Ironically this was a year after Freud announced his abandonment of hypnosis.)

Schultz too found that hypnotized patients reported heaviness in their arms and legs and a pleasant sensation of warmth as their stress was relieved. Like Vogt, he also found that patients could be taught to put themselves into this agreeable and recuperative state without a hypnotist.

Schultz combined Vogt's system with some borrowings from yoga and described his new system in a book titled *Autogenic Training,* which was published in German in 1932. Since then the book has gone into at least ten other German editions and has been translated into Spanish, Norwegian, French, Japanese, and English.

Schultz's colleague and coauthor, Wolfgang Luthe, MD, now works both in Montreal and as scientific director of the Oskar Vogt Institute at the medical school of Kyushu University, in Japan. Although the Greens are the most active supporters of autogenic training in the United States, others, including some medical-school faculty, have been looking into its clinical applications.

Schultz and Luthe's claims for the clinical benefits of autogenic training are so sweeping that they can be regarded only with the utmost caution and skepticism. Three ten-minute periods of training a day are said to bring about, in two to eight months, improvement or cures in psychosomatic disorders such as bronchial asthma, constipation, cardio-spasm, and sleep disorders. Behavioral and motor disorders that have been reported as successfully treated include writer's cramp, nocturnal enuresis, anxiety states, and phobias.

Among other problems that are said to yield in some measure to autogenic training are indigestion, peptic ulcer, ulcerative colitis, tachycardia (rapid heart beat), angina pectoris, myocardial infarction, high blood pressure, hemorrhoids, tuberculosis, diabetes, low back syndrome, and various sexual disorders.

Psychotherapeutic applications cover virtually the entire spectrum of neurotic and psychotic disturbances. Finally Luthe states that autogenic training increases the body's resistance to all kinds of stress.

As if this were not enough, Luthe also reports substantial social and emotional benefits. Social contact is said to be less inhibited and more natural, with both intimacy and autonomy being encouraged.

Autogenic training is also said to be useful in high-stress situations, such as combat, interrogation, and life in prisoner-of-war camps. At the end of one's life autogenic training is recommended in connection with "nirvana therapy," in which a person suffering from a clinically hopeless disease is eased into the hereafter.

Autogenic training is almost as simple to learn as transcendental meditation. First, the trainee relaxes as thoroughly as he can in a place as free as possible from distractions. He may be lying down, half-reclining in a comfortable chair, or sitting slumped. He closes his eyes.

When he is comfortable, the trainee is directed to repeat silently a series of "standard formulas." The first is "My right arm is heavy" (for right-handed people). At the beginning this exercise should not be carried on for more than thirty seconds to a minute. As training goes on and the patient is introduced to other training exercises, the period of passive concentration grows to a half hour or so. Care is needed, for Luthe warns that distressing psychic effects—crying spells, feelings of loneliness, and depression—can follow ill-advised efforts. One should not, among other things, try too hard.

The standard training exercises are directed toward producing sensations of heaviness and warmth, a slow and regular heartbeat, slow and regular breathing, a feeling of warmth in the abdomen, and coolness of the forehead. Once the trainee gains some experience, the exercises are reported to produce immediate results.

A substantial common element is clearly shared by autogenic training, relaxation through self-hypnosis, and transcendental meditation. The most striking difference between autogenic training and TM is that in TM the mantra is deliberately meaningless while in autogenic training the phrases are directed toward specific results.

If autogenic training stopped at curing diarrhea, general feelings of nervousness and sweaty palms, it would not challenge our acceptance, for the effectiveness of its highly structured exercises is not beyond the bounds of the often demonstrated power of suggestion. But our willingness to believe becomes less and our resistance grows when Schultz and Luthe proceed from the standard exercises to what they call "organ-specific formulae," which are directed toward particular disorders, such as hay fever, hypertension, tuberculosis, glaucoma, angina pectoris, hemorrhoids, and even an itchy vulva.

The organ-specific formula for the last disagreeable condition is "My vulva is cool." The formulas for more threatening disorders are equally simple. For tuberculosis the formula is "My lungs are warm"; for hay fever, "My nose is cool"; for glaucoma, "My eyes are cool"; and so on.

Clearly we have stepped over the line of easy belief. Glaucoma is a disease of the eyes characterized by increased pressure within the eyeball, often leading to blindness. If it can be alleviated by repeating the formula "My eyes are cool," we have entered a world in which our thinking about disease and healing must undergo a substantial revision.

Before we turn away in disbelief, however, let us remind ourselves of two facts. First, medical science does not know the cause of glaucoma. Second, not even the most skilled ophthalmologist can cure glaucoma, but only discourage its destructive progress. Among the standard recommendations for treatment is the avoidance of emotional stress.

Luthe recommends many other organ-specific formulas for specific disorders, all to be used carefully under the supervision of a therapist after the trainee has mastered the standard exercises.

For coughing the OF (as he abbreviates organ-specific formula) is "My throat is cool, my chest is warm."

For bronchial asthma, he recommends either (1) "My throat is cool" or (2) "My chest is warm" or (3) "It breathes me. . . . It breathes calm and regular."

For hypertension Luthe prescribes, "My forehead is agreeably cool. My head is clear and light" or "Heartbeat calm and easy." He prescribes the last phrase for angina pectoris also.

For trouble in sleeping: "Warmth makes me sleepy. It sleeps me. Waking does not matter. It sleeps me."

In addition to these organ-specific formulas Luthe also recommends what he calls intentional formulas (IF), which he describes as a specific type of mental support that helps the trainee in his effort to deal successfully with some mental and physical problems. Among the most potentially useful of these are the "abstinence formulas" to help overcome alcoholism and cigarette smoking.

The IF for alcoholism is "I know that I avoid drinking a single drop of alcohol, in any form, at any time, under any circumstances, in any situation; others drink, but for me alcohol does not matter."

For cigarette smoking, the IF is "I know that I avoid smoking a single cigarette, at any time, under any circumstances; others smoke, but for me cigarettes do not matter."

An informed critic of autogenic training is Dr. Neal Miller of the Rockefeller University (formerly the Rockefeller Institute), who is a formidable figure in the scientific world of operant conditioning and biofeedback training. Interested in autogenic training's claims of producing beneficial changes in heart rate and blood pressure, Miller organized two groups of subjects, one of which practiced autogenic training and the other of which practiced what he called "anti-autogenic training."

"The autogenic training group used the exercise that their hands were getting heavy and warm," Miller told me. "The anti-autogenic group used the exercise that their hands were getting light and cool." The expected result was that the autogenic group would decrease their heart rate and blood pressure, while the anti-autogenic group would do exactly the opposite, increasing both.

This is what happened—and yet, curiously, the anti-autogenic group was much more successful, producing larger changes and producing them more reliably.

"The change in blood pressure wasn't high enough to be statistically reliable," Miller said, "but we're absolutely sure of the heart rate, which averaged a difference of five or six beats a minute." Miller wasn't quite sure why the results turned out the way they did, but there was no question that autogenic training, whether pro- or anti-, brought about measurable changes in the workings of the body.

Another informed critic of autogenic training is Johann Stoyva, an experimental psychologist at the University of Colorado Medical School. An articulate young man with straight yellow hair and a neat blond mustache, Stoyva took his PhD at the University of Chicago, working under Dr. Joe Kamiya, who is generally credited with the discovery of alpha-wave biofeedback.

Stoyva became interested in autogenic training through a chance remark made by a subject in a series of experiments in the posthypnotic suggestion of dreams. "My first subject was a girl from Germany," he recalled. "She told me, 'You know, with your interest in hypnosis, dreams, and so forth, you really ought to look up the literature on autogenic training.'

"Well, I sort of had the idea that experimental subjects can't tell you anything, but about six years later I looked autogenic training up and I started thinking that if you put these things together—autogenic training and behavior therapy and Jacobson and biofeedback—it might evolve into something useful."

Pursuing this line of thought, Stoyva went to Montreal to train with Luthe for a month. Luthe, he found, was "sort of defensive" about the hypnosis component, hoping that autogenic training would be accepted as a medical tool without being associated with the "spooky hypnosis area." Yet, as Stoyva found out, in Germany the scholarly associations for autogenic training and for hypnosis hold joint meetings.

Stoyva believes that autogenic training is not heterohypnosis—hypnosis by another person. "Distinguishing it from autohypnosis is a little tougher, since it grew out of autohypnosis," he said recently. "I guess the way I would look at autogenic training is this," Stoyva told me. "It has two major components. To begin with, it *is* training. You learn to do something—to relax, to shift your body into another condition, and to me it seems more parsimonious to consider that simply as learning rather than as hypnosis.

"But as it's used clinically, I think there's also an element of autohypnosis in autogenic training. The formulas for the various disorders seem to me to come directly from autohypnosis." He went on to say that he was still puzzling over whether to look on the training phrases as strictly a "learning-training" thing or whether to think about them as autosuggestion.

"Let me tell you a couple of other things about these phrases," Stoyva went on. "Take standard exercise one, '*My right arm is heavy.*' After you've been training about a month with the heavy-and-warm exercise, you end with repeating '*I am at peace, I am at peace.*'

"But Luthe doesn't start you out with that I-am-at-peace thing. I think what he and Schultz hit upon is an important learning principle. If you use the phrase only when you're profoundly relaxed, it becomes associated with relaxation, and it then becomes a conditioned stimulus for relaxation. I think this is a valuable feature of their approach."

Studies made at a number of laboratories, mainly in Germany, have borne out the claim that autogenic training does influence the functions of the body in an immediate and direct way. Like transcendental meditation, autogenic training decreases the heart rate, blood pressure, respiratory rate and respiratory volume. Also like TM, autogenic training is associated with the production of alpha and theta waves.

This similarity is not surprising. Both practices are forms of yogic concentration, and both partake of a large measure of hypnosis (whatever hypnosis is). Both are something more than simple relaxation.

The key to autogenic training, according to Dr. Luthe, lies in its tendency to help the body normalize its own functioning. As the trainee concentrates on such a phrase as "My hands are warm" (so goes the argument), changes occur in his autonomic nervous system that cause the capillaries in the surface of his hands to expand and carry more blood. His hands consequently become warmer.

The relaxation can either be general (and measurable in terms of heart rate, blood pressure, or galvanic skin response) or it can be directed toward the operation of some organ or function by invoking the "organ-specific" formulas. The body undergoes readjustment, asserts its own wisdom, and the physical and mental disorders tend to correct themselves.

The trainee can defeat his purpose by trying too hard. In fact, Luthe has said that one of the most important elements in the autogenic approach is the trainee's "casual and passive attitude." Similarly the instructor of TM will warn his student not to "push the mantra," for trying too hard can bring on headaches and other disagreeable consequences. A bit of Zen is surely visible in both these cases.

As ways of letting go, Zen, yoga, hypnosis, transcendental meditation, and autogenic training are remarkable more for their similarities than for their differences. All are based on the principle of passive concentration, whether on a meaningless phrase or on a specific suggestion. All can cause measurable changes in the functions of the body that respond to stress. All work.

## SURVIVAL MANUAL: LESSON THREE

*Hand-Warming*

Among the various techniques of letting go, hand-warming is one of the simplest, most direct, and most effective.

Tape-record the following instructions, which were developed at the Menninger psychophysiology laboratory and are based on Schultz and Luthe's "standard formulas." Speak slowly and deliberately into the microphone, leaving long pauses between the phrases.

Here are the instructions:

"I feel quite quiet. . . .

"I am beginning to feel quite relaxed. . . .

"My feet feel heavy and relaxed. . . .

"My ankles, my knees, and my hips feel heavy, relaxed, and comfortable. . . .

"My solar plexus, and the whole central portion of my body, feel relaxed and quiet. . . .

"My hands, my arms, and my shoulders feel heavy, relaxed and comfortable. . . .

"My neck, my jaws, and my forehead feel relaxed. . . .

"They feel comfortable and smooth. . . .

"My whole body feels quiet, heavy, comfortable and relaxed.

"I feel quite relaxed. . . .

"My arms and hands are heavy and warm. . . .

"I feel quite quiet. . . .

"My whole body is relaxed and my hands are warm, re-laxed and warm. . . .

"Warmth is flowing into my hands, they are warm . . . warm."

Now sit down where you will be comfortable. Take your finger temperature and write it down. Rewind the tape and play it back to yourself.

Listen to each phrase and then repeat it to yourself silently. As you say, "My feet feel heavy and relaxed," imagine that your feet are turning into sacks of cement. As you say, "My arms and hands are heavy and warm," imagine your hands lying in a pan of soapy, steaming water. When the tape is through, take your finger temperature again.

Don't be surprised or distressed if at first your temperature shows no change or actually goes down. Don't try to force the results. Play the tape every day—better yet, play it morning and evening—always remembering to take your finger temperature before and afterward. In a few days you will find that the temperature *is* rising—two degrees, four degrees, six degrees, and eventually as much as ten degrees.

You will also find that as your hands warm up, your sense of tension will go down. You have learned to let go.

After you have had some success in warming your hands, you will find that you won't need the thermometer because it will be perfectly clear to you that your hands are becoming warm. And finally you may find that you don't need to repeat any phrases at all but can warm up your hands simply by imagining them in warm water.

One of the great advantages of this technique is that you can use it anywhere—at home, at your desk, riding a commuters' train at the end of the day, or even in the midst of a business meeting in which the tensions all around you are beginning to rise.

## Hypnosis and Relaxation

If you have learned to warm your hands, you have learned to hypnotize yourself.

Here is another method, suggested by Dr. Cheek, who believes that all hypnosis is self-hypnosis. The hypnotist, Cheek says, is merely a guide.

Some people will need the help of such a guide to learn to put themselves into hypnosis. Others will find that they go easily and naturally into a state of hypnotic relaxation. If you succeeded in warming your hands, you can probably learn to hypnotize yourself by this method, which is adapted from instructions given by Dr. Cheek.

Tape-record the following instructions, speaking clearly, slowly, and confidently. Leave pauses long enough to allow you to follow each instruction.

"Make sure you are comfortable. Flex your wrists and your ankles. Roll your head around on your shoulders. Close your eyes. Take two or three deep breaths.

"Repeat mentally the following suggestions:

*"Now I am going into hypnosis.* (Pause.)

"Then three times slowly repeat the phrase *Relax now.* (Pause.)

"As you repeat this, you will begin to slip into hypnosis.

"Now you will want to go deeper.

"Imagine yourself on an escalator. You are going to ride the escalator down, down, down. As you go down, you will go deeper and deeper into hypnosis.

"Step onto the top of the escalator. As you ride downward count backward from ten to zero. Step off at the bottom when you reach zero. (Pause.)

"Any time you want to go into a deeper stage repeat the escalator technique.

"When you are ready to awaken yourself, you should think *Now I am going to wake up.* (Pause.)

"Count slowly to three, and you will then awaken, always feeling refreshed, relaxed, and clear-headed on awakening."

Now rewind the tape recorder and follow the instructions. You will succeed the first time in achieving some relaxation, but don't expect too much. Like everything else worth doing, it takes practice to learn to relax easily and quickly through hypnosis. You will not go into any sort of mysterious trance, but you will feel loose, and relaxed, and at peace.

If you have trouble sleeping at night, follow the instructions as you lie in bed. Repeat the escalator technique several times if you have to. The odds are very good that you will drift off to a more than usually refreshing sleep.

## Controlling Pain

If you learned to relax through the hand-warming technique or the escalator technique, you can learn to control pain.

Let us start by assuming that you want to rid yourself of the annoyance of a very minor but persistent pain such as a mosquito bite on your hand. First, relax by whatever technique works best for you—*shavasan*, meditation, or hypnosis.

Then concentrate on the pain of the bite. Examine it. Try to think of the itching as a rather interesting sensation. It isn't something that you need to be troubled by. It doesn't really matter. You are not obliged to suffer.

Imagine that your hand is becoming numb. It is not going to have any more feeling than a cold lump of clay. It is no longer even part of you, but is turning into something "out there."

Now imagine that you have a row of light switches in the middle of your head. Find the switch that controls the sensations from your hand. If there is any itching left, you can get rid of it by turning off the switch. Turn off the switch. The itching will disappear entirely.

Learning to dismiss pain is a skill. Like all skills, it is learned in small steps. Start with the next minor pain that happens to you. Relax. Let go. Examine the pain. Put it "out there." Turn off the switch.

Once you have become expert at coping with small pains you will find that the same technique is effective with bigger pains—even with a thumping toothache. You may not be able to remove the pain of the toothache entirely but you can reduce it to a minor discomfort that you can live with until you get to your dentist. And once you are in the dentist's chair, you can lie there relaxed, without any major discomfort, and without any fear or apprehension.

Our attitude toward pain is complicated by our cultural and family conditioning, by the sense of guilt that is instilled in us as children, and by our perverse need for punishment. For these reasons particularly, learning to control pain is not easy. But there is no question that it can be done. Remember that even terminal cancer patients have been trained by hypnosis to cope with their otherwise dreadful pain, and to live out their days comfortably, serenely, and with dignity.

# 5

# Letting Go with Biofeed-back

## BIOFEEDBACK AND AUTOGENIC TRAINING

IN 1967 the Greens embarked on a series of experiments aimed at testing the effectiveness of autogenic training by itself and when reinforced by biofeedback. Their intention was to carry the work of Schultz and Luthe "one step further by combining the conscious self-regulation aspect of yoga and the psychological method of autogenic training with the modern instrumental technique called physiological feedback."

Biofeedback is an application to physiology of the lessons of the cybernetics revolution. In the process of biofeedback a person is shown, through sensitive instruments, changes going on in some bodily function as they actually occur. It has been demonstrated again and again, that if a person can see, for example, his heart rate change, he can learn to raise or lower it at will.

The Greens had become convinced of the effectiveness of autogenic training in an experiment in which they had tried to teach thirty-three Topeka housewives to develop physiological control, particularly of their skin temperature. As Green describes the results, "Some of the ladies failed to achieve much temperature control, but a couple of them succeeded so well that we decided to continue studying autogenic training."

They decided to see if they could increase the effectiveness of autogenic training by combining it with biofeedback, and enlisted eighteen college men, whom they tried to train

simultaneously to reduce the muscle tension in their
forearms, increase the temperature in their hands, and increase the percentage of alpha waves in their EEG recordings.

The feedback of these three bodily processes was displayed to each student by the movement of three vertical
bars of light on a panel. He was told to try to relax completely
and achieve zero muscle tension, to increase the skin temperature of his right hand by ten degrees Fahrenheit, and to
produce 100 percent alpha rhythm over a period of ten seconds. Whenever he managed to achieve any of these conditions, the corresponding bar of light rose to its full height of
five inches. When he failed to do so, the bar of light disappeared.

The students were trained in using the feedback meters
and then instructed to repeat silently such autogenic phrases
as "I feel quite quiet," "My feet are heavy," and "My ankles,
my knees, my hips, feel heavy and relaxed."

Some of the students found they could achieve unusually
low levels of muscle tension in a single session. One of them
told the Greens, "I felt I was floating above the chair."
Another said, "I'm sort of light like. I'm not even sitting here.
I feel like I'm just detached in some way." A third said,
hesitantly, "It sounds funny, but . . . well, okay . . . it seems
like there was some kind of force on the inside, flowing
through my forehead out . . . not a hard pressure but you
can feel it, like when you move your hand through flowing
water."

The most striking result in controlling the warmth of his
hand was turned in by one of the students who had already
had some experience in yoga. He could change his hand
temperature by ten degrees in two and a half minutes while
watching the feedback meter. The rest of the students succeeded in raising their temperatures an average of three
degrees after three or four sessions.

In percentage of alpha waves produced, the average student increased his production from 24 percent to 45 percent.

In summing up the experiment the Greens had to admit that they had expected too much in setting the students the task of simultaneously mastering three physiological variables. Most of them learned to control one or another function quite well, and some learned to control two functions simultaneously, but nobody learned to control all three at the same time.

From this and similar experiments the Greens learned that autogenic training alone was not nearly as effective as biofeedback alone. Excellent results were obtained when the two methods were combined.

Another important lesson echoed Schultz and Luthe's insistence on passive, rather than active, concentration. Whenever a subject tried to raise his temperature, it invariably went down. But if he relaxed and told his body what to do and observed the results in a detached way, his temperature would rise.

The subjects also experienced most interesting long-term results that went beyond what they had learned in the Greens' laboratory. They began to improvise new methods and work out techniques that proved to be best for themselves.

As Elmer Green recalls this discovery, "It's interesting that as soon as we combined biofeedback with autogenic training, people would use the phrases for a couple of days and then would start using their own visualizations. For instance, they may find that if they were warming up their hands and had learned how to do it a little bit, they actually found out that as they were saying the warm phrases they would begin to think of warm water. Pretty soon they wouldn't use the phrases any more and would just switch to warm water, and that seemed to work just as well. Then finally the last stage, the voluntary control stage, which they get into when the meter is taken away—they either continue their own visualization or else they just tell their hands to get warm and forget it, and then their hands get warm."

By comparison with any other method of learning to con-

trol our bodily processes at will, biofeedback training offers
the most effective instrument in achieving results quickly
and regularly.

This does not mean that hypnosis, transcendental meditation, and autogenic training have at one stroke been super-
seded and rendered without value. Hypnosis is still the
method of choice in reducing pain without drugs. Transcendental meditation still offers a ready way to achieve serenity
without using either mood-changing drugs or expensive instruments. Autogenic training still offers a means of coping
with stress-related physical and psychological disorders.

Biofeedback, however, gives us a method of dealing directly with the functional disorders that afflict human beings, short-circuiting periods of training that may extend
from weeks to months to years. Green and other workers in
the field now believe that a person can learn to regulate to
some degree any of his bodily processes that can be displayed
to him.

At one laboratory or another people have been trained to
self-regulate their blood pressure, blood flow, heart rate,
lymph flow, muscle tension, and brain waves. Asking himself
where the limits to self-regulation will be found, Elmer
Green answers, "Nobody knows, but research indicates that
the limits lie much farther out than was at first suspected by
most of those interested in biofeedback."

## HEADACHES

A headache-ridden twenty-nine-year-old research technician at the University of Colorado Medical Center, a married
but childless woman, became the first patient trained in
biofeedback muscle relaxation in the laboratory Johann
Stoyva shares with Dr. Thomas Budzynski. (Like Stoyva,
Budzynski is an experimental psychologist in the department
of psychiatry.)

The technician-patient, whose initials are S.E., suffered

frequently from headaches—not migraine but tension headaches, which are brought on when the muscles of the neck and scalp contract painfully. "Muscle-contraction headache" is a more accurate but less-used term. It is also called a depression headache or psychogenic headache because it is a response to stress.

S.E.'s headaches had started when she was nine years old and had continued ever since. The pain was usually located toward the front of her head and on both sides. When they occurred, the headaches came on gradually, starting in the morning and continuing all day.

After a medical examination had ruled out the possibility that S.E.'s headaches had an organic or neurological origin, Budzynski and Stoyva started her on a course of training based on their earlier observations that experimental subjects receiving feedback from their forehead muscle (which anatomists call the frontalis) had reported they had learned easily to relax not only the frontalis but also other muscles of the body, particularly in the head. Since the pain of tension headaches come from the contraction of the head muscles, the two psychologists reasoned that if their patient could be taught to relax these muscles, her headaches would become less painful and gradually disappear.

S.E. was wired up to an electromyograph (or EMG), an instrument that measures the electrical voltages in the muscles. When muscles are tense, they produce relatively high voltages. (The electrical potentials involved are on the order of a millionth of a volt.) When muscles relax, the voltages drop. There is no electrical activity when the muscles are completely relaxed.

The EMG produced two outputs—a digital readout for the investigators and a varying tone in the earphones that S.E. wore. When her frontalis muscle generated a relatively high voltage, S.E. heard a high-pitched tone. When her frontalis relaxed, the pitch of the tone became low.

In schematic outline, the feedback circuit looked like this:

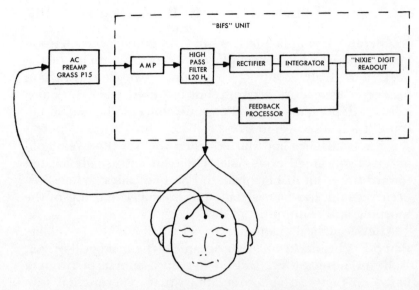

Fɪɢ. 1. Functional diagram: EMG information feedback.

The principle of feedback appears in this laboratory setup in one of its simplest forms. If the earphones were taken away, S.E. would have no way of knowing whether her frontalis was tense or relaxed. When she listens to the earphones, however, she is given very precise information about the state of tension of her frontalis at that exact moment.

Furthermore, if she changes that state of tension, she is immediately told the direction and degree of change. If the tone of the signal becomes rapidly higher, she knows that her frontalis is becoming rapidly more tense. If the tone of the signal becomes slowly lower, she knows that her frontalis is slowly relaxing.

As Stoyva remarked to me when I visited him in his laboratory, "The single most powerful principle of learning is knowing right away how you've done."

This is precisely how S.E. learned to manage her headaches.

Before they began feedback training, Budzynski and Stoyva discovered that, as they had expected, S.E.'s baseline

EMG readings were about twice as high as a normal person's. After feedback training was introduced, S.E. would report for two or three sessions of half an hour each two or three times a week. As she became more expert, silent sessions, without feedback, were occasionally interspersed, the point being to help free her of dependence on the machine.

She also practiced relaxation at home every day and kept a daily record of her headaches. These record cards showed that S.E.'s headaches were worst on Mondays and Thursdays and least troublesome on weekends. The most certain cause of a headache was meeting her supervisor in the early afternoon, and these headaches were also the most painful. Other headaches were brought on by minor incidents such as forgetting a shopping list, losing the keys to her car, or having to make dinner for company.

Besides the EMG training, the experimenters gave S.E. some common-sense advice, suggesting that she try to ward off those afternoon headaches by relaxing in her chair during the lunch hour.

S.E. herself first reported that she felt some improvement during the third week of training, but the lab records showed that her EMG level had actually started to drop during the first week. She continued the training for a total of nine weeks, during which both the EMG readings and the frequency and painfulness of her headaches declined steadily.

S.E. came back to the laboratory for a follow-up interview three months after her EMG training had ended. She told Budzynski and Stoyva that her headaches had virtually disappeared. The investigators could find no sign of what psychiatrists call symptom substitution, with some other reaction to stress taking the place of the headaches.

Like other study subjects in the Denver lab, S.E. reported that she was becoming more sensitive to the rising tide of tension inside herself and that she could now cope successfully with it. The others too said they no longer overreacted to stress and that things just didn't bother them as much as they used to.

A follow-up study verified the results of Budzynski and Stoyva's first attempts to use biofeedback to relieve tension headaches. A number of people in this experimental group had been taking large doses of antiheadache drugs and tranquilizers. After EMG training, their daily use of drugs dropped remarkably. A person who had been taking four Valium every day stopped taking drugs entirely. Another dropped from four Darvon a day to none.

Budzynski and Stoyva interpreted the lack of success in some cases as underlining the psychic and social elements that make a headache a useful lever to move other people to do as you want them to do.

The migraine headache and the tension headache are two different things entirely, as every sufferer from migraine can testify. Migraine is a violent and paroxysmal headache that is often accompanied by disturbances of the vision and of the gastrointestinal system.

The onset of migraine may be signaled by depression, irritability and restlessness. The pain is often general but sometimes afflicts only one side of the head. Nausea and vomiting are common. The arteries of the scalp may be visibly enlarged and throbbing. The migraine may occur every day or only once every several months.

In spite of heroic efforts medical science has failed to cope with the migraine. Measures to ward off this disabling headache include protein injections, artificial fever, special diets, hormones, histamine, sedatives, and operations on the arteries of the scalp. But, as a widely used physicians' manual observes of these remedies, "None is specific, and relief depends largely on the enthusiasm of the physician and the patient's confidence in him."

Once an attack is under way, there is little the doctor can do except to dose the patient with aspirin, codeine, and ergot derivatives. Migraine is truly a wretched and miserable affliction.

About four blocks from the University of Colorado Medi-

cal Center, Budzynski and Dr. Charles Adler, a young
psychiatrist, operate a private clinic for sufferers from migraine. They use biofeedback as their anchor technique, along
with such other procedures as hand-warming, relaxation
training, and psychotherapy.

Budzynski, who is a dark-haired, casually dressed, relaxed
young man, explained to me the differences between tension
headaches and migraine headaches. "When a person is put
under stress, there's an increase in muscle tension, and that's
when the tension-headache person is likely to get his pain,"
Budzynski said. "The migraine-type person gets it on the
rebound, when the stress is over with and when he's relaxing.
There's a compensatory increase in blood-vessel size in the
arteries of the head, and, unfortunately for the migraine
person, the compensatory reaction is too much. The arteries
are distended to the point where they no longer have the
elastic properties they should, and therefore the pain sensors
are activated with each pulse of blood through them."

Budzynski and Adler consequently try to help the patient
cope with migraine by changing himself (or, more likely,
herself) in two directions. First, EMG relaxation training
with feedback teaches the patient to react less violently to
stress. The patient is also taught hand-warming techniques
to use as an emergency measure if they are unexpectedly
caught in a highly stressful situation. Secondly, the problem
is approached psychologically through therapy that gives the
patient a better insight into himself.

Budzynski stressed to me the importance of using both
physiological and psychological training, citing as an example the case of an attractive young married woman who had
come to the clinic for relief from migraines that were being
nourished by situations at home.

Mrs. X had problems both with her children and her husband. She used her migraines in the classic ploy to avoid
making love to her husband; she used them to keep her
husband from going out at night; and she used them to avoid

going to parties. As Budzynski commented, "You can see how headaches can become a terrific weapon for some people, and they're very reluctant to give them up."

"We had to alter her physiology and we had to go through a lot of behavior therapy with her," Budzynski went on. "The sexual situation worked out all right. They were healthy, attractive people who'd been doing things the same way ever since they were first married—the straighforward missionary position—and they'd grown bored with each other." Budzynski set them to reading *The Sensuous Couple* and they discovered it was fun doing things a little differently.

There was still the problem of the headache Mrs. X developed when she had to go to a party or soon after she arrived. These headaches turned out to be due to the fact that, although she was a more than usually attractive woman, Mrs. X had not had as much formal education as the other women in her social circle, who out of jealousy for her good looks frequently put her down conversationally. The therapists trained her to be more assertive and to value her own opinion more highly.

"She's a much nicer person to be around now," Budzynski said. "Her headaches have really decreased, but I don't think they would have if we hadn't worked on some of those other problems. The headaches were too important to her before that. They served her quite well."

"And that's why you can't use biofeedback in a vacuum," Budzynski concluded.

I asked about the relationship of the EMG biofeedback training and the hand-warming techniques.

Budzysnki said these were two tools working toward the same end. "We think maybe it's a more complete program than the training at Menninger," he said. "Elmer Green and the others there use autogenic phrases which do have relaxation properties and these do help in the relaxation phase of things. We just think the results can be improved with EMG feedback."

At Menninger, Dr. Joseph D. Sargent (the chief of internal

medicine), Elmer Green, and their associates have been using feedback together with autogenic phrases to tackle migraines that have failed to yield to other methods. They do not use psychotherapy but center their method on the feedback of hand temperature.

The method was discovered by lucky chance. A subject who was being trained simultaneously in EEG feedback, EMG feedback, and controlling the blood flow in her hands by autogenic training happened to suffer from migraine. When she succeeded in raising the temperature of her hand ten degrees Fahrenheit, the migraine went away. Two other migraine sufferers in the experimental group asked the investigators to let them try the hand-warming method also. It worked completely for one of them and gave some relief to the other.

A study of seventy-five other headache sufferers followed. These people not only took part in training sessions at the laboratory but also used portable temperature trainers at home. They were encouraged to try to get along without the trainer; after a month most of them found they didn't need it at all.

Three quarters of the group was found to be improved after a minimum follow-up period of a year. The results were much better with the migraine sufferers than with those who were afflicted with tension headaches.

Sargent and Green concluded cautiously that their experiment was not intended to exclude other methods of headache control, such as medication and psychotherapy, but that they thought that a severe migraine headache could be brought under control more quickly if the hand-warming exercise was used in addition to medication.

The dean of American researchers in biofeedback, Neal Miller, also advises caution in interpreting such experimental results. "It's known that there are spontaneous fluctuations in migraine," Dr. Miller told me when I visited him recently. "This introduces a statistical artifact. A person suffering from migraine is likely to come in for treatment at the peak of the cycle rather than at the trough. This means that on the average migraine sufferers seem to get better after seeking treatment. There's also a genuine placebo effect. Their hopes are raised, and this may help them get better."

Evidence on the positive side comes from the Chicago Medical School, where Dr. Seymour Diamond, who is president of the American Association for the Study of Headache, has tried both temperature and EMG feedback on about two hundred patients.

Starting as a "big doubter of Budzynski's work," Diamond bought an EMG apparatus and worked with patients with whom everything else had failed. To his surprise and his patients' gratification, Diamond found that both hand-warming and EMG training worked pretty well—hand-warming helping 25 percent and EMG feedback helping 40 percent of the sufferers.

It also helps to be young, Diamond found out. The success rate went down markedly with patients over thirty years old.

Migraine is not the only disorder for which hand-warming has been used. At Menninger, Dr. Sargent has taught hand-warming to victims of Raynaud's disease, in which the small blood vessels of the fingers go into spasm, cutting off the circulation. The consequences may include gangrene. The results so far have shown that hand-warming helps if it is started early enough.

"But once Raynaud's symptoms begin, and the patients' hands feel numb or turn pale, they can't warm their hands anymore," Sargent has reported. "They have to learn to predict situations in which they'll develop symptoms and warm their hands prophylactically. If they can do this, they can stay out of trouble."

## FEEDBACK AND PHOBIAS

Whenever an architect with the initials J.L. drove home after dark, he imagined there was a corpse in the back seat of his car. He fell apart inside whenever he was confronted by such images of death as funeral parlors, graveyards, coffins, and corpses. His fear of the dark became so incapacitating that he could no longer go into the darkened basement of his house.

Hoping to rid himself of his death phobia, J.L. volunteered as a subject for Stoyva and Budzynski, who in the early 1970's were proceeding on a new tack—the "desensitization" of phobias through a combination of behavior therapy and biofeedback. (In general terms behavior therapy addresses itself to immediate results, directly attacking undesirable behavior patterns rather than trying, as psychoanalysts do, to go to the root cause. Behavior therapy is much faster and is much cheaper.)

Guessing that they might have some success with phobias by substituting a relaxation response for an anxiety response, Budzynski and Stoyva started by giving J.L. alpha-feedback training. In the first two sessions he learned to increase his alpha level from 20 percent to 80 percent.

J.L. was then asked to imagine four death-related scenes and to rank them in order of the anxiety they caused him. (The four scenes were, in ascending order, sleeping in the attic, a cemetery, a coffin on the train, a body in the coffin.)

J.L. was then wired up to the alpha machine again and told to visualize the four scenes but to remain relaxed, with the alpha feedback giving him a clue to his state. However, the experiment was not entirely successful because as soon as J.L. began to visualize any scene, pleasant or unpleasant, his alpha rhythm simply disappeared. The patient asked them to keep on with the alpha feedback, however, because he felt it did help him relax.

At the end of four days J.L. could visualize each of the scenes without anxiety for at least twenty seconds. Even more important, his desensitization to these particular scenes had the effect of reducing his fear of darkness and death in general. When he came back six months later for a checkup, he reported that he was no longer afraid of going into dark places.

Budzynski and Stoyva decided to try EMG feedback instead of alpha training in the treatment of phobias. Their decision was supported on the foundation laid by Dr. Joseph Wolpe's work in behavior therapy. Put simply, Wolpe's thesis is that a person who is in a state of muscular relaxation cannot suffer from acute anxiety.

The EMG machine used was similar to the instrument they had used with tension headaches. The patient usually first receives training in relaxing his frontalis because Budzynski and Stoyva think that relaxing the frontalis tends to relax the entire body. If the frontalis doesn't work for a particular patient, the electrodes are moved to the masseter (a jaw muscle) or the extensor muscle of the forearm.

Even the tensest patient can make a little progress with feedback from the masseter or the forearm muscle. A little progress then leads to further progress. As an aid to behavior therapy, feedback has the great advantage that it allows the relaxation training to be broken down into small steps.

In practice the patient relaxes through EMG feedback until he reaches a suitable level. The therapist then tells him to imagine a pleasant scene. As the session proceeds, the therapist monitors the patient's progress by means of a light display. So long as the EMG level remains below the criterion that has been set for the patient, the light is green. If the patient begins to tense up, the light turns amber. If the tension becomes extreme, a red light goes on and the therapist ends the session.

A typical patient was a woman who had reached a point of no progress with her behavior therapist, who sent her to Budzynski and Stoyva. Her trouble was that she was overcome by terror in social situations. At a party her hand would tremble so strongly that she couldn't shake hands or hold a glass.

Feedback with the frontalis muscle produced only disappointing results. The electrodes were moved to her forearm, then to the masseter, and then back to the frontalis. The procedure worked and the woman learned to relax physically. She then went back to her regular therapist, who, without using further feedback, desensitized her, which is to say he relieved her of her symptoms. She now goes to parties without anxiety and her hand no longer shakes.

In the course of work such as this, Budzynski and Stoyva made a most extraordinary discovery. Working with patients who were instructed to press a switch as soon as they felt anxiety, they found that these signals lagged behind the EMG's indicator of anxiety by about five to fifteen seconds. In other words the body was aware of stress long before, relatively speaking, the mind became aware of it.

Pursuing this controversial observation, the investigators found that in every case they tried, the EMG response was more sensitive than the subject's own report. The very best of their subjects could not signal his own awareness of anxiety until five seconds after the EMG had reported that his anxiety was rising.

Budzynski and Stoyva's discovery bears on the ancient body-mind problem and recalls the proposition put forward many years ago by William James that psychological effects follow rather than precede physical effects—that we feel sorrow *because* we cry, and that we experience fear *because* we run, and not the other way around. It also recalls the great truth that guided Walter B. Cannon: The body has a wisdom of its own.

## VISCERAL LEARNING

The most impassioned leader of the biofeedback revolution—for, surely, it is a revolution in our way of thinking about our bodies—is Neal Miller, who has remarked with feeling upon the "ancient, strong and invidious" prejudice against the autonomic nervous system and who has described laboratory results as freeing man "from the shackles of viewing the autonomic nervous system and visceral functions with contempt."

In spite of rhetorical flourishes such as these, Dr. Miller is an exceedingly hard-nosed scientist who sees biofeedback training in terms of operant conditioning, which is also known as Type II conditioning, instrumental learning, and trial-and-error learning.

The range of behavior that can be taught by operant conditioning is limited only by the experimenter's ingenuity and the responses his subject is capable of making—which is to say that not even the most talented experimenter can teach a pig to fly, but he *can* teach a pigeon to play Ping Pong, as B. F. Skinner did in a famous experiment at his laboratory at Harvard.

The essential thing that happens during operant conditioning is that the subject is promptly rewarded whenever by chance it makes the desired response. One cannot ask a pigeon to hit a Ping Pong ball with its beak. One can, however, reward it with a grain of corn whenever it just happens to hit a ball that has been bounced in its direction.

Similarly, one cannot instruct a man to lower his blood pressure with much hope of success. One can, however, reward him by flashing a blue light whenever his blood pressure just happens to dip down for a moment. As Miller has put it, "Such a signal serves to reward the visceral responses just as the success of seeing a long, straight drive rewards a correct stroke in golf."

As the learning process goes on, the desired response happens more often. Eventually the pigeon learns to play Ping Pong instead of hitting an occasional ball, and the man learns to control his blood pressure.

Operant conditioning is by no means accepted as a good thing by all the scientific workers in biofeedback training. Elmer Green regards it as close to a philosophic evil, and argues instead for the virtues and benefits of what he calls "voluntary control." Green has expressed his view of the matter plainly: "Voluntary control moves toward increased inner freedom; conditioned control moves toward loss of inner freedom." Yet it does not seem to me that what Green does in Topeka and what Miller does in New York are so very different.

Now in his middle sixties, Miller graduated from the University of Wisconsin, took an MA at Stanford, and then a PhD at Yale. Since leaving the Yale faculty in 1966 he has worked at the Rockefeller University. He has received many of the honors that come only to the most eminent of our scientists.

While at Yale, Miller and his colleague Leo DiCara carried out a classic experiment in which rats that had been paralyzed by curare were taught to perform such feats as causing one ear at a time to blush. At Rockefeller he has broadened his investigations in the operant conditioning of visceral processes to human beings from the nearby New York Hospital-Cornell Medical Center. It is quite a leap from a laboratory rat to a human being suffering from, say, high blood pressure, but as Miller has put his view of the matter, "I believe that men are as smart as rats, although we may not yet be as clever at training them as we are at training rats."

Miller and DiCara have trained rats to increase and decrease their heart rates, blood pressure, urine formation, saliva secretion, the contraction of their intestines, and the patterns of their EKG and EEG. As Miller has pointed out, teaching an animal to control his organs can change the betting odds on whether the animal lives or dies. Or as DiCara has put it, "If visceral responses can be modified by instrumental learning, it may be possible in effect to train people with certain disorders to get well."

To the psychologist there is a crucial difference between operant conditioning and the classical conditioning developed in the late 1800's by the great Russian psychologist Pavlov in his well-known experiments with salivating dogs. In 1965 at Yale Miller and DiCara undertook their now-celebrated series of experiments with curarized rats to demonstrate that there are no real differences between the two kinds of learning and that the same laws apply to learning voluntary (or "skeletal") responses and involuntary (or "visceral") responses.

The rats were paralyzed with curare in order to rule out the possibility that learned skeletal responses would interfere with the desired visceral response. Curare is the arrow poison used by some South American Indians to paralyze their prey. It is also used in the operating room to relax the muscles, as in abdominal surgery.

A curarized rat cannot, literally, move a muscle. The striped muscles that move the legs, chest, head, and tail become flaccid and useless, but the smooth muscles of the heart and the gastrointestinal and urinary systems continue to function.

The rat cannot breathe and must be kept alive in a respirator. It cannot eat and must be rewarded in some other way. Miller and DiCara consequently planted electrodes in the pleasure centers of the rats' brains. When the rats produced the desired response, they were rewarded with a slight pulse of electrical current that produced presumably ecstatic feelings.

The experiments demonstrated dramatically that curarized rats could be taught to change their bodily functions in whichever way the experimenters wanted. If the experimenters rewarded the rat whenever its heart rate increased, its heart rate would continue to increase. If they rewarded it when its heart rate decreased, its heart rate would continue to decrease. If they rewarded it when its right ear flushed pink, its right ear would continue to flush. If they rewarded it when its left ear flushed, its left ear would continue to flush. If they rewarded it when its blood pressure rose, its blood pressure would continue to rise. If they rewarded it when its blood pressure dropped, its blood pressure would continue to drop.

The experiments were a triumphant success in validating Miller's hypothesis. Furthermore, they raised the clear possibility that human beings could learn to control their heartbeat and blood pressure just as the rats had. As Miller put it, the question was whether non-curarized men were as good at visceral learning as are curarized rats.

There is no final answer yet from Miller's laboratory. An attempt to apply the principles of visceral learning to a woman suffering from high blood pressure showed promising progress and then came to an inconclusive end. And then, from workers in other laboratories who had tried to reproduce the Miller-DiCara experiments, came the disturbing news that the curarized rats were no longer learning as they had at Yale.

On a bright spring day in 1973 I met Miller at his office and had lunch with him at the university cafeteria, looking out over the East River. While waiting for him, I noticed that on the wall of his outer office hangs a now-fading color photograph of Miller shaking Lyndon Johnson's hand as he received the National Medal for Science in 1965. His secretary, a middle-aged lady with a British accent, suggested to me that the yellowing photo might someday be replaced by one of Miller receiving the Nobel prize.

Miller is a heavy-set man who looks more like a beer-drinking truck driver than a laboratory scientist of extraordinary and subtle ingenuity. He is quite bald, but his eyebrows sprout vigorously and his conversation is direct and lively. He walks with a swinging gait like a sailor ashore.

Over a bowl of soup, Miller talked about his disappointments both with the curarized rats and with the hypertensive patient. Nothing Miller or his assistant, a graduate student named Barry Dworkin, or his old colleague Leo DiCara could think of had any success in making the rats behave the way they had before. The rats' heart rates ran 10 to 20 percent higher than they had been and they stayed high. Miller changed his brand of curare. It did not help. He changed his strain of rats. There was no change, and the rats simply continued to resist learning.

Miller found himself in the classic nightmare situation of the scientist—to have carried out an elegant and productive experiment only to find out that neither he nor anybody else can reproduce it. As Miller has remarked mordantly, "The problem is that whereas there often are millions of ways of doing something wrong, there may be only one or two ways of doing it right."

As matters stand now, Miller occupies the uncomfortable position of knowing that his original experiments may not have demonstrated what he thought they demonstrated and that his curarized rats may not actually have been learning. When I asked him how he felt about these earlier experiments, Miller answered, with just a touch of grimness, "I still have considerable confidence in the old results. They seem to be very robust."

Miller's disappointment in repeating the experiments with the curarized rats is not the only experience that has moved him to take up a position of great caution. As he told me, "The press has picked up information coming out of our laboratory and has gotten people's hopes up. It's extremely important to have controls for placebo effects. Some people, for instance, will bring down their blood pressure after receiving medication that is nothing but a sugar capsule. This may help the patient, but it doesn't do much for the scientist who's trying to learn how to teach the patient to control his blood pressure."

Miller went on to talk about the inconclusive outcome of the case of Robin Bielski, a patient with high blood pressure who was trained by Miller and Dworkin to lower her blood pressure at will. (The Bielski case is described in detail in Gerald Jonas' fine book *Visceral Learning*.)

In the spring of 1970 Robin Bielski, a thirty-two-year-old woman who worked as an advertising copy writer in New York, was taken by ambulance to the New York Hospital-Cornell Medical Center suffering from an undiagnosed but sorely troubling complaint. For the better part of a week she had been suffering from overwhelmingly painful headaches that made her so dizzy she was afraid to leave her apartment.

The examinations at the hospital finally led to the conclusion that Miss Bielski had suffered a cerebellar hemorrhage. She was operated on and the hemorrhagic swelling was removed.

When Miss Bielski regained consciousness after a long

coma, her left side was largely paralyzed. After an interlude at her own apartment, where her mother cared for her, she entered New York University's Institute for Rehabilitative Medicine. Her condition was alarming. Her blood pressure rose from 180/110 to 230/140 before being stabilized by drugs at about 150/100.

Miss Bielski's doctor knew about the work going on at Miller's lab and thought it might provide a solution to the problem of her persistently high blood pressure. Barry Dworkin interviewed her and reported back that she seemed to be a first-rate candidate. A couple of weeks later Miss Bielski was initiated into the learning process, which, it was hoped, would teach her to lower her blood pressure and to keep it at a low level.

She learned while she lay on a cot in a dark room, with a blood pressure cuff around her upper arm. A microphone sensed the flow of blood. Electrodes were attached to her body to record other vital processes. Whenever her blood pressure changed in response to Dworkin's suggestions, she heard an electronic *beep*. This was the reward, or reinforcement, for correct performance. Dworkin would ask her to lower her blood pressure, to raise it, or to hold it steady. When she did as she was asked, she would hear the *beep* of approval.

Before long, Miss Bielski had learned to reduce her diastolic pressure as low as 70. Her doctor approved Miller's request that she be taken off her antihypertensive drugs. Her pressure went up for several days and then went down again.

Her case was going so well that Miss Bielski was allowed to leave the hospital and move into a new and more conveniently located apartment. Under the pressures of taking care of herself while getting around in a wheelchair, her blood pressure rose. Then it dropped again. She continued to report to Dworkin at University Hospital. She eventually learned to control her diastolic blood pressure over a range of 29 mm., from 65 to 94.

The case of Robin Bielski seemed to be on its way to being

a world-recognized landmark not only in experimental psychology but also in the treatment of high blood pressure. If one woman could learn to reduce her blood pressure from a dangerously high reading, then so could millions of other people suffering from this pervasive, life-threatening illness.

The essential process was simplicity itself. Miss Bielski's account of what went on in her mind recalls the reports of people learning yoga, autogenic training, transcendental training, and self-hypnosis. The patient, who had in fact already studied yoga, reported that the only way she could sustain a drop in blood pressure was to clear her mind of all stressful thoughts, to let go completely, and to imagine her brain as a lake lying inside her head.

There was another element in Miss Bielski's training that was reminiscent of the Eastern disciplines and the importance they place on the teacher, the master, or the guru. Dworkin and his patient established a close teacher-learner relationship that most evidently had a great deal to do with her success. Miss Bielski compared him to an Olympic coach and wrote, "I feel we are friends and allies—it's really as though *we* were lowering my pressure."

And then, just when the investigators seemed to have success in their hands, it slipped infuriatingly from their grasp. Miller is not sure yet which of a succession of events interfered most critically with Miss Bielski's ability to keep her blood pressure down.

It is clear she went through some unsettling experiences. She underwent an operation to correct a squint in her left eye that was a leftover from her cerebellar hemorrhage. She went on a Caribbean cruise with a friend and discovered how really restrictive her physical condition was and how little chance she had of ever leading a normal life.

When she came back from the cruise, her diastolic pressure was in the nineties. She went back on medication. She tried visceral training again, but it didn't work. (This time, however, it was supervised not by Dworkin but by somebody else.)

As Gerald Jonas remarked in his meticulous account of the case, "But what is not yet clear . . . is whether she has lost *all* voluntary control of her blood pressure or whether her control was simply not strong enough to overcome the effects of the constant stress she has been subjected to in recent months. (The fact that a man collapses under the burden of a five-hundred-pound weight does not prove that he cannot lift a two-hundred-pound weight.)"

When I asked him what had happened to Robin Bielski, Miller told me that she had just come back to his laboratory and that her pressure was high again. She had not entirely lost the ability to control it, but it worked largely in the wrong direction since she could raise it about 15 mm. but could lower it only about 5.

Miller looked more than usually grave and said, "To take the worst possible view, we may have taught her to lower her blood pressure only when the physician was measuring it. Then, because of her apparent improvement she was taken off drugs. Perhaps by doing this, we did permanent damage to her."

I remarked that there must be many traps to be avoided before the experimenter can be sure of a result that will stand up. Miller nodded and said that when dealing with the hypertension problem, there were at least two phenomena that produced results that looked favorable but were really quite accidental.

First, he said, because the patient has a feeling of hope, he (or she) stops worrying, which has a favorable effect on blood pressure. Second, the patient gets to know the person who regularly takes his blood pressure, and as his familiarity grows and his apprehension goes down, so does his blood pressure.

"We noticed with one female patient that whenever a physician took her blood pressure in his office it was high; whenever a technician took it in the lab it was low," Miller said. "You *could* interpret this to mean that something was happening in the lab that was effective in reducing her blood pressure, but in fact she just felt more at ease in the laboratory than she did in the doctor's office."

He went on to describe another problem that was bothering him, the possibility that he and his assistants were training their subjects to lower their blood pressure just at the moment it was being measured. As soon as the cuff was taken off it might go right up again. There are ways of measuring the blood pressure constantly, such as with automatic cuffs like those the astronauts wear. "But this is a thing you hesitate to do because it calls for a portable device that takes the blood pressure through a catheter in the artery," Miller said. "It's been done in England, but it's nothing you want to do lightly."

Several months after my visit I wrote to Miller, asking what progress he had been making with these problems. He replied with a one-sentence letter, which read, "We are still having trouble with the curarized rats but, with future treatment, Robin Bielski's blood pressure appears to have been reduced again in spite of the fact that she is gradually being taken off most of the drugs."

Research in teaching people to control their hearts and blood vessels is by no means confined to Miller and the Rockefeller University. As far back as 1962 Dr. Peter J. Lang at the University of Pittsburgh was teaching people to make their hearts beat faster or slower. He called it teaching them to "drive" their hearts because the training apparatus looked like a driving-skill game in a penny arcade.

Lang continued his work later with students at the University of Wisconsin. When Lang asked the students how they learned to drive their hearts, they had trouble trying to explain what went on inside. We all, in fact, have trouble describing what goes on in our bodies. As Lang put it, "I am just as inarticulate in trying to describe the muscles and movements I use in making a forehand shot in tennis as my subjects are in describing how they control their heart rates."

Just as Hilgard's student-subjects had done in his hypnosis experiments, Lang's students had made up their own mental routines, counting backward or thinking of emotional events. Some of them developed peculiar ritual movements that they superstitiously thought changed their heart rates.

At the Harvard Medical School Herbert Benson, David Shapiro, Bernard Tursky, and Gary E. Schwartz found they could teach blood-pressure patients to reduce their pressure through operant conditioning and feedback. Their subjects were seven middle-aged patients at Boston City Hospital who had been diagnosed as suffering from essential hypertension. The patients were paid five dollars a session to sit quietly and do nothing while their blood pressure was measured by an automatic cuff. Their feedback reward included lights, sounds, the flashing of a photographic slide of a pleasant scene, and reminders of the amount of money they were earning.

Five of their seven subjects learned to lower their blood pressures substantially, the range going from 16.1 mm. to 33.8. As the Harvard researchers pointed out cautiously, however, all they had proved was that blood pressure could be lowered in the laboratory, not necessarily anywhere else.

Drs. Jasper Brener and Roger A. Kleinman have obtained similar results at the University of Tennessee. Undergraduates were given direct feedback of their systolic blood pressure through a pressure gauge and were told to try to reduce the reading through mental processes. They were given no other clues as to what they were supposed to do.

In spite of this absence of any instruction the students managed to drop their average blood pressure from about 131 mm. to about 115, for an average change of 16 mm. Another group of students, who were not given feedback, actually registered a slight increase in their blood pressures.

EMG feedback from the frontalis muscle appears to work with blood pressure just as it does with tension headaches. At Nova University in Fort Lauderdale, a group of patients trained by Dr. William A. Love, Jr., lowered their mean blood pressure from 153/100 to 135/88 in sixteen weeks.

Dr. Love believes that there may be two things going on

—the first is that as the muscles relax generally, there is less muscular pressure on the small arteries. The other possibility is that if a person manages to keep his general level of tension low, less energy goes into the hypothalamus, which controls a number of bodily functions, including blood pressure.

The most consistently encouraging work in this general field is probably that of Dr. Bernard T. Engel at the Gerontology Research Center of the Baltimore City Hospitals. Since he started this work at the University of California in the mid-1960's, Engel has worked with patients suffering from cardiac arrhythmias—which is to say dangerous disturbances in the rhythm of the heartbeat.

Among these arrhythmias is a condition known as premature ventricular contraction (or PVC). Patients suffering from PVC complain of skipped heart beats, choking sensations, and a feeling that "something has turned over" in their chests. PVC's are life-threatening and increase the probability of sudden death.

Engel and his colleague Theodore Weiss set out to see if patients with dangerous PVC's could be taught to control their heart rates. The apparatus they used was a bank of three lights at the foot of the patient's bed. Like traffic lights, they were red, green, and yellow.

The red and green lights told the patient to slow down or speed up his heart. The yellow light told him that his heart had responded correctly. As he became more expert, the feedback was gradually phased out and the patient taught to depend on his own sensations to tell if he was doing the right thing.

One of the most successful patients was a fifty-two-year-old woman, L.R., who had had five myocardial infarctions during the preceding thirteen years, three of them in the year before she joined the study. Her doctor had put her on quinidine to suppress her PVC's, but had had to take her off the drug because it caused persistent diarrhea. Without the quinidine L.R.'s PVC's increased from one or two per minute to about ten per minute.

Using the traffic-light apparatus, L.R. soon learned to increase or decrease her heart rate at will. The object of course was to learn to keep her heart rate regularly low, since this also reduced the number of PVC's. (She told the experimenters that when they asked her to speed up her heart, she thought about relaxing; when they asked her to slow down her heart, she concentrated on breathing maneuvers.)

After about twenty sessions with the traffic lights L.R. learned to keep her heart rate in the comfortable range of 60 to 70 beats per minute. The frequency of PVC's dropped to one every five minutes, and then one every ten minutes. Her doctor took her off all medication and she was discharged from the hospital.

During the following months L.R. demonstrated that she had indeed learned to control both her heart rate and the life-threatening PVC's. When she felt PVC's, she sat down and rested, putting herself in the state she had been trained to in the hospital. The PVC's would stop and not return. Best of all, she had apparently escaped from the threat of another myocardial infarction.

Dr. Engel is confident that he has shown the way for cardiac patients to control their hearts and lengthen their lives.

## ALPHA

Of all the biofeedback phenomena, the apparent ability of people to learn to control the waves produced in their brains has created the greatest public stir and has been the most thoroughly misunderstood. About five years ago magazines began to hail the arrival of the drug-free electronic "high," advertisements for training equipment began to appear in the classified departments of such sober journals as the *New Republic, Psychology Today,* and the late *Saturday Review.* And astonishing claims began to be made by those who stood to profit by this new shortcut to a fulfilled life. The greater focus was on the benefits of the alpha wave, but there was interest in the theta wave as well.

The literature of a reputable manufacturer of alpha-feedback equipment declares that his apparatus has been used successfully for brain-wave control, meditation, classroom demonstrations, phobic desensitization, pre-therapy relaxation, prisoner rehabilitation, as a drug alternative, in ESP research, for curing stutterers, to help hyperactive children, in studies in creativity, to reduce tension, in training athletes, in studies of learning, and to slow the entire autonomic system. Commercial mind-training courses that have capitalized on the alpha fad go even further.

Alas for this brave new world, in June, 1973, the Food and Drug Administration announced that it was looking into the claims of the alpha promoters with a cold eye. Dr. Joseph Davis, head of the medical devices division, declared that the firms involved were "making pretty wild claims for psychological and health benefits that can't be supported by any studies we have seen." Furthermore, Davis said, a considerable number of the machines that were being sold to the public weren't feeding back alpha waves at all but only vibrations produced in their own electronic circuitry.

The alpha and theta waves, however, remain a matter of serious interest at a number of our leading research institutions and it seems clear that EEG feedback is a useful approach to the management of stress.

The alpha wave and the other brain waves were discovered and named by Hans Berger, an Austrian psychiatrist who in the 1920's found that sensitive recording equipment (which was later named the electroencephalograph, or EEG) could detect the presence of exceedingly small voltages in the brain.

Berger noted that these voltages oscillated regularly —which is to say that they produced wavelike shapes when plotted on paper—and ranged from a slow frequency of one cycle per second to a relatively rapid frequency of about thirty cycles per second, which is half the frequency of household electric current in the United States. The voltages are very small, in the range of 10 to 100 microvolts. It would take the collective voltage produced by all the citizens of Duluth, Minnesota, to light up one six-volt flashlight bulb.

Berger divided the brain waves into four groups, identifying each with a Greek letter.

| Delta | Theta | Alpha | Beta |
|-------|-------|-------|------|
| 1—3.5 | 4—7 | 8—12 | 13—30 |

Frequency in cycles per second (Hertz)

Delta is produced during deep sleep. The theta wave occurs during deep reverie and is thought by some people, such as Elmer Green, to be the state in which artistic and intellectual creation takes place. Alpha is associated with a state of calm relaxation, and is prominent in the brains of Zen masters and yogas during meditation. Beta accompanies the state of ordinary, eyes-open attention.

Since Berger's discovery, the EEG has been used by neurologists and psychiatrists as a diagnostic tool and by laboratory workers as a powerful device for exploring the activity of the brain. Epilepsy, for example, shows up on the EEG in the form of great paroxysmal spikes that seem to mean that the distressing symptoms of epilepsy are produced by an electrical storm in the brain.

Neal Miller has been interested for many years in the possibility that operant conditioning using biofeedback might be effective in teaching epileptics to control the electrical hurricanes that produce their seizures. Together with his colleagues A. Carmona and Julius Korein he has cautiously reported some success.

Stronger evidence that epileptics may find relief from biofeedback training has come more recently from the work of Dr. Maurice B. Sterman, who is chief of neuropsychology research at the Sepulveda VA Hospital and associate professor of anatomy at the UCLA medical school. Working with cats, Dr. Sterman discovered that when the animals were absolutely motionless, they produced a rhythm of 12 to 14 cycles per second, a frequency just a little higher than the alpha wave (8–12 cps). He trained his cats to produce this rhythm, which he called SMR (sensorimotor rhythm), at will. Whenever they did, they froze into absolute still lifes.

Making one of those leaps of imagination that often lead to surprising discoveries, Sterman set out to see if people suffering from epilepsy could be trained to produce SMR and if this ability might help them avert their terrible seizures. After working with five epileptics over a period of two years, Sterman found that their brain-wave patterns were moving in the direction of the normal, and particularly that the dramatic paroxysmal electrical discharges that produce *grand mal* seizures were becoming fewer and fewer.

One young woman benefited most strikingly from SMR training. Whereas she used to average two seizures a month, she had only seven during the eighteen months after she began training. In the last six months of the period she had only one seizure.

EEG biofeedback research goes back only to the late 1950's. While doing sleep research at the University of Chicago (where Johann Stoyva was one of his assistants), Dr. Joe Kamiya became interested in a technical problem: Could his subjects tell him when they were producing alpha?

A subject lay in a cot in a dark room, with electrodes running to an EEG in an adjacent part of the lab. Every once in a while a bell would ring. The subject's task was to tell whether or not he was producing alpha. He would be told immediately whether he was right or wrong.

"The first day he was right only about 50 percent, no better than chance," Kamiya reported. "The second day he was right 65 percent of the time; the third day, 85 percent. By the fourth, he guessed right on every trial—400 times in a row."

This extraordinary outcome changed the direction of Kamiya's professional life and turned him into the world's leading authority on EEG feedback. A Nisei born in Turlock, California, Kamiya took three degrees, culminating in the

PhD, at the University of California in Berkeley. He is a rather short, round-faced man, nearing fifty, who talks intensely and without stopping.

"My excitement in the field has been theoretical—not curing people of their headaches," Kamiya told me when I visited him in the rather untidy little house where he does his work on the edge of UC's San Francisco medical center. He made a grimace of distaste and went on. "I've done precious little work since my first experiments. I seem to spend all my time raising bread and getting my people to work together in the lab." He added rather dourly that the Nixon administration's throttling of research funds had hit him hard.

Since the early 1960's Kamiya has been at the Langley-Porter Neuropsychiatric Institute, an autonomous institution that is physically part of the great university medical center that overlooks Golden Gate Park. His work here has been directed toward finding out whether or not people can actually control their brain waves.

Kamiya set up a simple feedback circuit to test the possibilities. Whenever alpha waves were recorded in the EEG, an electronic device gave out a characteristic tone.

When the tone was first heard, Kamiya would say to the subject, "Hear that tone? That's turned on by your brain wave." After letting the subject rest and relax for a while, Kamiya would say, "Now let's see if you can learn to control the percent of time that the tone is present. First we'll have you try and keep the tone *on* as much as you possibly can, and then we'll have you try to keep the tone *off* as much of the time as you can."

The experiment worked. Kamiya quickly discovered that people could learn to control their brain waves, producing or suppressing alpha as he asked them to. He also found there was a close connection between the alpha state and the visual imagination. The more a person imagines something in visual terms, the less alpha he produces.

Kamiya was also interested in how his subjects described

their sensations while in a high-alpha state. He found that people who meditated or who were introspective by nature learned easily to produce high percentages of alpha. Alpha also comes easily to people who have become interested in such personal growth techniques as sensitivity training.

Other good learners were people who enter readily into personal relationships. Kamiya discovered a correlation between his personal liking for people and their aptness in learning alpha control. He once reported with a straight face, "I find this especially true of females, for some reason."

The 1960's were the decade of the great alpha boom, with Kamiya's first report leading a parade of publications by other experimental psychologists in Russia and England as well as in the United States. One of these others, Edmund Dewan of the Air Force's Cambridge Research Laboratory, is remembered in the annals of alpha research for having achieved such a finely tuned level of control that he could transmit Morse-code messages through his alpha waves.

Elmer and Alyce Green have pointed out sensibly that there really is no such thing as training in brain-wave control. Instead the subject is really being trained in maintaining certain states of feeling that happen to be accompanied by the desired brain-wave patterns. (The same comment applies equally well to heart-rate or blood-pressure training.) Nobody really produces alpha. Instead he produces a state of mind that he has been told goes along with alpha.

These cautionary remarks are very much to the point, for the enthusiasts and promoters of alpha training have claimed that a seventy-dollar feedback device (an electroencephalophone or EEP) opens the door to instant yoga.

This claim is not entirely fanciful. EEG studies of yogas have, as we have seen, demonstrated they do produce high levels of alpha during meditation. Whether the converse is true, and a high level of alpha is identical with the yogi's meditative state is a question that is harder to answer.

It may help us to reach a realistic balance between the claims and the reality by considering the case of the eight cats whom researchers at the Veterans Administration Hospital at Sepulveda trained to generate slow EEG patterns for a food reward. Did these animals go into a yoga state? It is an interesting question, but it seems unlikely that it will be answered.

People who have learned to produce alpha have, however, given us copious and detailed reports on their subjective experiences. Kamiya's subjects who had also meditated told him that the alpha state was close to the mystical state. Another reported an inner visual field "like a flowing gray-black film with a luminous quality."

Johann Stoyva describes the mental state of about half his subjects as "content-free consciousness" marked by the absence of visual imagery and a sense of tranquility. The alpha state and a state of emotion are apparently incompatible; Stoyva has reported that in his own experience any twinge of emotion causes alpha to vanish.

While working with David P. Nowlis at Ernest Hilgard's laboratory at Stanford, Kamiya asked the subjects to describe their internal state when they tried to produce both high and low levels of alpha. For high levels the answers included letting go, relaxing, letting the eyes go out of focus, floating, and imagining pleasure, security, and warmth. For low alpha the reported states were alertness and vigilance, tension, agitation, "holding on." Other subjects answered that they had no idea at all how they either induced or suppressed alpha.

Probably the most ambitious claim for the alpha state has been made by Durand Kiefer, a professional naval officer who has devoted his retirement years to the investigation of altered states of consciousness. Kiefer has said that he experiences great joy whenever he meditates with alpha feedback, and that when his meditation goes on for several hours he enters a state resembling the Christian state of grace that continues for twenty-four or forty-eight hours.

At the Sepulveda veterans' hospital Dr. Barbara B. Brown explored the connection between alpha and the subject's perception of his mental state. A blue light was the feedback signal. When alpha waves were present, the light turned on. When the alpha waves grew stronger, the light became brighter. The subjects were asked to identify the internal feelings that made the light become as bright as possible.

The most successful subjects turned out to be those who let go completely, "dissolving in the environment" or losing a-wareness of everything except the light. The alpha state, in other words, is subjectively the same as the state experienced by meditators or people who have relaxed deeply under hypnosis.

We may consider this finding in two ways: Either training in producing alpha leads to a pleasing sense of empty relaxa-tion or, conversely, the achievement of a pleasing sense of empty relaxation can be identified through an alpha-feedback device. So far as the practical benefits go, it does not make much difference.

Some of these practical benefits have already become ap-parent. Alpha feedback is another means, parallel to Zen, yoga, meditation, and autogenic training, to relieve the mind for a while of its excess baggage and to induce profound relaxation. Whatever benefits come from deep relaxation will come from alpha-training also. But alpha is nothing in itself; it is only an indicator that the desired state has been reached. As Dr. Eleanor Criswell of Sonoma (California) State College has put the matter neatly, "If you have alpha," she says, "it may mean a good state or it may just mean eight to twelve cycles per second."

Although some exploratory work has been done in using alpha training in the management of such conditions as epilepsy and stuttering, not enough clinical work has been done to lead to any definite conclusions.

"I haven't seen any convincing evidence that alpha has any direct clinical usefulness," Joe Kamiya told me. "But I have a hunch it's going to be useful."

I asked if he could describe some of the directions in which the usefulness might go.

"First, there's all this longstanding stuff on meditators and correlations with Zen masters and yogis," Kamiya said. "The yogis say it's good for you. The Zen people don't say it's good for you—they just say do it. The important thing seems to be the letting go that seems to go with producing alpha—letting go of your critical faculties just as you do in meditation and hypnosis.

"Second, I think alpha's going to turn out to be useful in psychotherapy." He smiled and added wryly that nailing down the usefulness of psychotherapy itself was sort of hard. Then he went on, "I've come to the belief that alpha-feedback training will be useful mainly to help the patient to get to first base. In working with alpha subjects I get the feeling there's this kind of letting go of defense mechanisms and defended thinking."

He added that in the laboratory he found that people who produced alpha easily entered into personal relations with him more easily and weren't so busy keeping themselves at a distance.

Kamiya stopped talking and peered intently at me for a moment. "How many letters in Minnesota?" he asked.

I thought for a moment, looked to my left, and then, looking back at Kamiya, guessed eleven.

Kamiya laughed. "It doesn't matter. You answered my question when you looked to the left. You see, people in whom the right half of the brain is dominant tend to look to the left, and people in whom the left hemisphere is dominant tend to look to the right. Right-lookers tend to be analytical, while left-lookers are intuitive and integrative. Right-lookers don't learn alpha easily. Left-lookers do. That's interesting, isn't it? There's good reason to think that this laterality question will be important in the future understanding of biofeedback processes."

Part of Kamiya's future research—provided he gets the funds he needs—is going to be devoted to finding out more about left-right dominance.

Even broader horizons for alpha-state research have been described by Elmer Green and Gardner Murphy. Murphy has declared that it is an urgent matter to find out whether the voluntary control of alpha and theta waves can act to clear away our defensive tensions and "the whole intricate world of self-deception."

Green sees a relation between the alpha and theta states and the states in which artistic and intellectual creation takes place. Green likes to tell the story of the nineteenth-century German chemist Kekule Von Stradonitz who discovered the structure of the benzene ring in a reverie in which he saw a snake swallowing its own tail. Perhaps, he suggests, other people can learn to have such inspirations.

So far, this attractive proposition remains only a hypothesis. Whether, as Green hopes, training in producing alpha and theta waves can enhance the creative powers of people with unrealized potential remains to be demonstrated. He is continuing work in this direction in his Topeka laboratory and, with his characteristic high spirits, has reported that Menninger's present feedback system is so sophisticated that "we sometimes claim that we are going to use the machine to train a subject to play 'The Star Spangled Banner,' with the hope that it will encourage the federal government to release additional funds."

## SURVIVAL MANUAL: LESSON FOUR

### Alpha Training at Home

As we have seen, the production of alpha waves is associated with a state of deep relaxation, of letting go. It would follow from this that the alpha-wave trainer for home use offers a direct and scientifically valid way to learn how to let go.

This may very well be true for you. Or it may not. The alpha-wave trainer for home use is not a magic instrument. The less-expensive models run about seventy dollars. Others run to several hundred dollars. Before investing this money, it will be worth your while to find out if there is a center near you where alpha training is offered. If there is a university or large college near you, you may find that researchers there are looking for experimental subjects. (Phone the department of psychology and talk to the secretary who answers.)

More likely you will find a commercial alpha-training or mind-training center. These vary widely in quality and honesty. Try to find one that offers group instruction, that doesn't make dramatic and overinflated claims, and that charges a reasonable fee. Buy a machine only after trying it out under these circumstances.

Using an alpha-feedback machine is very simple. The model I own is the standard Electroencephalophone (EEP-4) manufactured by J & J Enterprises of Bothell, Washington.

The EEP consists of a set of stereo earphones with an electronic package a little larger than a pack of cigarettes mounted on top. There are controls for sensitivity and for background noise. Two silver disk electrodes plug into the package. The source of current is a battery of the sort that is used in transistor radios. There is no danger of shock.

To use the alpha trainer, I first put an elastic headband around my head. Then I put a dab of electrode paste on the surface of each electrode and slip them under the elastic, one behind my ear and the other on the back of my head.

I put on the earphones, plug in the electrodes, and adjust the sensitivity and background controls. Until I plug in the electrodes I hear a steady humming sound that is produced by the EEP itself; when the electrodes have been plugged in, the sound changes. A sort of formless fluctuating noise represents random electrical waves. A steady *ssssh-ssssh-ssssh* indicates alpha. (Other makes of electroencephalophone give a warbling signal.)

Using the EEP I have discovered that I produce more alpha when I meditate than when I don't. I suppose that if I had bought the EEP *before* I learned to meditate, I would have learned to increase alpha by feedback alone. This, of course, has been demonstrated again and again by other people in strictly controlled laboratory experiments.

If I wanted to invest some more money, I could buy for about thirty-five dollars a percent-of-alpha meter, which would give me feedback showing the percent of time during which I succeeded in producing alpha. I would then have an approximate equivalent of the equipment that is used in many laboratories.

I am not, however, enthusiastic about home alpha training as a means of learning to let go.

To begin with, the publicity alpha training has received has gone far beyond the benefits that can be demonstrated.

Secondly, there is a good deal of dishonesty and half-honesty in the field, both among manufacturers and the operators of "mind control" training courses. Some of the machines don't feed back alpha at all but instead register voltages in the scalp muscles, which may or may not be a useful thing to learn to control. And, as the FDA has noted, some of the machines are outright frauds.

Finally, the other methods of letting go—breathing, meditating, autogenic hand-warming, and hypnosis—offer a greater range of possibilities for useful application.

Using a home alpha-wave trainer can be an interesting experiment. It can also help you learn to let go. But when you use an EEP, you should remember Dr. Criswell's incisive observation: "If you have alpha it may mean a good state or it may mean just eight to twelve cycles per second."

## Practicing Survival Techniques

These survival manual lessons have necessarily been something like a smorgasbord—a plate of this, a plate of that, and no main course anywhere to be seen. This approach is due to the nature of this book, in which we have explored several different frontier paths, each one leading in approximately the same direction, but each one quite separate from the others except at certain points of intersection.

This is all very well so far as the book goes, but it isn't very helpful to the reader who wants some advice on what to do in order to increase the odds on his own survival. One could, I suppose, practice Shavasan on Sundays, transcendental meditation on Mondays, autogenic training on Tuesdays, hypnosis on Wednesdays, and so on, but it would be a remarkably frustrating experience as well as an unproductive one.

What each of us needs to do, then, is to sample the various disciplines and then pick the one that agrees with us best. If your experiments with hypnosis seem to get you nowhere, simply forget hypnosis and try instead to master autogenic hand-warming or Shavasan or some form of meditation. They are all paths to the same destination.

When you have decided which road you are going to follow, try seriously to master the technique. It will not take much of your time and the rewards will more than repay you.

Practice regularly. Once a day is a minimum. Twice a day is better. Each session should take about twenty minutes.

Don't meditate or practice Shavasan right after eating. Before breakfast is a good time for your first session. Before dinner is a good time for your second. (I meditate before breakfast and before going to bed. Meditating before sleeping isn't what the Maharishi recommends, but it works for me, and I sleep soundly through the night.)

Don't try too hard. "Passive concentration" is the watchword. Don't push against the river. Float.

Don't expect too much too soon. Your rewards will come in small installments.

Whichever path you choose for your main effort, try also to learn to control pain. If you want an artificial pain to test yourself against, use the Stanford method and put your hand into a pan full of ice cubes and water. It is a powerful thing to discover that (in Dr. Margolin's words) you have learned how to trigger your right to ignore pain.

Most importantly, as you go along with your chosen course of training in letting go, occasionally measure your heart rate, your breathing rate, and your finger temperature. Record the readings on the charts in Chapter 4. When you begin to see a consistent change in the right direction, you will know that you are not only on the right track but also that you have already succeeded in achieving results that will help you reduce the destructive impact of stress on your life.

# 6
# Horizons

A GREAT hole remains in our knowledge. No hard evidence is at hand to demonstrate that on the whole people who have learned to let go live healthier and longer lives than do their friends and neighbors. Such evidence is not easy to produce, for what is wanting is a long-term study of the medical and social histories of a substantial group of people who have learned to let go, as compared to a control group of people who are similar in every respect except they have not learned to let go.

Such a study would not be inordinately expensive but it would yield convincing results only after a period of many years. Let us hope that a bright young investigator in a school of public health or a medical-school department of preventive medicine will adopt such a project as the focus for his career. The promise is there, and such an investigation might well benefit mankind many times more than the work that led to, say, the heart-transplantation operation or even to the development of polio vaccine. At its worst polio was, considered statistically, only a minor disease, which, as Dr. Michae DeBakey has said of heart transplants, "from a scientific point of view they are not that significant. We are still waiting for the real breakthrough, which will be finding a way to *prevent* heart disease."

What we are considering now is a mode of prevention that may work against the entire spectrum of major diseases. We must caution ourselves that we are talking only about a possibility, but it is a possibility that demands to be explored. It holds promise of leading us to a way of life in which we are no longer terrified that we may die at an unnecessarily early age from heart disease, cancer, stroke, and diseases of the lungs, which represent only the first four causes of death in America.

The stakes are surely high enough to demand that we proceed forthwith.

What lies just over the horizon is the means of coping with stress on an organized and truly professional level. Our explorations during the course of this book suggest a number of possible directions in which such an effort might be organized.

The success of Dr. Edmund Jacobson's progressive-relaxation clinic in Chicago, Adler and Budzynski's headache clinic in Denver, and similar clinics elsewhere suggest that every town large enough to support a dozen doctors should also support a stress clinic. The staff of such a clinic would be prepared to train patients in the entire range of techniques of letting go—whether these are physical techniques (as in progressive relaxation) or are based on biofeedback, or are meditative exercises, or draw upon hypnosis and autogenic training.

Besides physicians and psychologists, such a clinic would be staffed by a new type of professional, the stress therapist, trained (as physical therapists are now) in a university medical center and adept not only in the techniques of relieving stress but also indoctrinated with a new conception of the relationship of disease and health.

Many different sorts of people will be referred to the stress clinic. Perhaps the largest number will be sent by their physicians because they are in danger of becoming actively ill through the operations of stress. Another group will be those who suffer from chronic diseases such as hypertension, diabetes, cancer. Others will be convalescing from acute diseases and from surgery, a period during which stress is particularly dangerous. In all cases the patient will be learning to take an active part—*the* active part—in bettering his own condition.

Besides training people—both "sick" and "well"—in the general relief of stress, the stress clinic will also offer courses of training directed to specific conditions. The way has already been charted by the headache clinic. Patients suffering from other and more severe disorders will benefit from similar training. High blood pressure, the incipient myocardial infarction, congestive heart failure and the cardiovascular diseases generally represent an area where the need is great and where we are on the verge of demonstrating success with stress-relieving techniques.

Even the management of cancer may fall within the purview of the stress clinic, with training in letting go serving as a supplement to the conventional triad of surgery, radiation, and chemotherapy. (Elmer Green, never reluctant to take a bold look ahead, has suggested that the remission of cancer may be encouraged by teaching the patient to cause the starvation of cancerous tissue through voluntary control of the blood flow.)

Letting go can become an even more integral part of our everyday lives through a minor addition to the school curriculum. The mechanism for teaching such an unconventional subject already exists in the state requirements that each child receive instruction in physical education and hygiene. Here is the appropriate place to include basic instruction in these life-preserving techniques. Just as they now learn the best way to brush their teeth or to throw a ball accurately, schoolchildren will learn to put themselves to sleep, to tolerate pain when it comes, to avert headaches, to feel genuinely at ease in difficult circumstances, and to ward off the life-threatening physical consequences of stress.

When such changes are first attempted, there will of course be opposition. Some will come from medical men who mistakenly interpret stress therapy as a threat to their ancient prerogatives, their place in society, and their incomes. Other opposition will come from social theorists disturbed by the implications of teaching "passivity."

The grounds for such an argument have already been stated by Joost Merloo, who has objected that "The cult of passivity and so-called mental relaxation is one of the most dangerous developments of our times. We cannot escape the tenseness and challenges that surround us without inadvertently giving in. Challenge and tension are part of life. People have to learn to cope with them adequately and to use their leisure time for creative and gratifying activities."

This is stirring stuff, but it is entirely misdirected. As we have seen, letting go is not a technique for slipping into a passive, all-accepting state, but rather it is a technique for mobilizing one's best energies for more effective action than would be possible otherwise. Dr. Merloo's position is essentially the puritan position that one must suffer in order to accomplish anything worthwhile.

It is surely true that in a puritan society more than enough obstacles and causes for suffering will be placed in the way of the creative person. Yet this does not have to be. There is another way, which is not the way of suffering and eventual destruction but the way of natural growth and accomplishment.

As Ch'i Po told the Yellow Emperor more than two thousand years ago, "Those who have the true wisdom remain strong while those who have no knowledge and wisdom grow old and feeble. Therefore the people should share this wisdom and their names will become famous."

There are personal and social implications in our understanding of this "true wisdom" that go far beyond the prevention or alleviation of physical suffering. The psychologist Gardner Murphy has argued that advances in feedback technology give us the means to bring new weapons to bear on the problem of self-deception and "discover *how* we are deceiving ourselves, and use much of the technical expertness of modern science in the process of looking inside us, as Socrates would have done if the tools had been available."

The Greens look forward to a "society of self-regulating individuals," while Joseph Hart has proclaimed the advent of a new cultural age in which man will learn to control his own consciousness through a combination of age-old techniques and modern technology.

For the present let us content ourselves with a more modest objective—to mobilize the wisdom of the body in the prevention of disease and the alleviation of pain. But as we concern ourselves with these immediate matters, let us not forget the greater discoveries yet to be made as we move beyond our present horizon.

The last word belongs to William James, still the greatest of American philosophers and psychologists, who said that the best way to encourage great new discoveries is "to understand how great is the darkness in which we grope and never to forget that the natural-science assumptions with which we started are provisional and revisable things."

# FOR FURTHER
# READING

*General*

Alexander, Franz, MD, *Psychosomatic Medicine: Its Principles and Applications.* New York, Norton, 1950 (paper).
Cannon, Walter B., MD, ScD, *The Wisdom of the Body.* New York, Norton, 1963 (paper).
Dubos, René, *Mirage of Health: Utopias, Progress, and Biological Change.* New York, Harper & Row, 1971 (paper).
Dunbar, H. Flanders, MD, *Mind and Body: Psychosomatic Medicine.* New York, Random House, 1947.
Luce, Gay Gaer, *Biological Rhythms in Human and Animal Physiology.* New York, Dover, 1971 (paper).
Selye, Hans, MD, *The Stress of Life.* New York, McGraw-Hill, 1956 (paper).
Weil, Andrew, MD, *The Natural Mind.* Boston, Houghton Mifflin, 1972.
Wolff, Harold G., MD, *Stress and Disease,* revised and edited by Stewart Wolfe, MD, and Helen Goodell. Springfield, Charles C. Thomas, 1968.

*Altered States of Consciousness*

Tart, Charles, ed., *Altered States of Consciousness.* New York, Wiley, 1969.
White, John, ed., *The Highest State of Consciousness.* New York, Anchor, 1972 (paper).

*Yoga*

Eliade, Mircea, *Yoga: Immortality and Freedom*, trans. from the French. Bollingen Series LVI, Princeton, 1969.
Wood, Ernest, *Yoga*. New York, Penguin, 1959 (paper).

*Zen*

Kapleau, Philip, *The Three Pillars of Zen*. Boston, Beacon, 1965.
Sato, Giei, *A Diary of Zen Monastic Life*. University Press of Hawaii, 1973.
Suzuki, D. T., *Zen Buddhism*. New York, Anchor, 1956 (paper).
Watts, Alan, *The Way of Zen*. New York, Pantheon, 1957.

*Meditation*

Naranjo, Claudio, and Ornstein, Robert E., *On the Psychology of Meditation*. New York, Viking, 1971.
Trungpa, Chögyam, *Meditation in Action*. Berkeley, Shambala Publications, 1970.
Yogi, Maharishi Mahesh, *Transcendental Meditation: Serenity Without Drugs* (formerly titled *The Science of Being and Art of Living*). New York, Signet, 1963 (paper).

*Hypnosis*

Cheek, David B., MD and LeCron, Leslie M. *Clinical Hypnotherapy*. New York, Grune & Stratton, 1968.
LeCron, Leslie M., *Self-Hypnotism: The Technique and Its Use in Daily Living*. New York, Signet, 1964 (paper).
Sparks, Laurence, *Self-Hypnosis*. Hollywood, Wilshire Book Co., 1962 (paper).

*Autogenic Training*

Luthe, Wolfgang, MD, ed., *Autogenic Therapy*, six vols. New York, Grune & Stratton, 1969.

*Biofeedback*

Barber, Theodore, DiCara, Leo V., Kamiya, Joe, Miller, Neal E., Shapiro, David, and Stoyva, Johann, eds., *Biofeedback & Self-Control: An Aldine Reader on the Regulation of Bodily Processes and Consciousness.* Chicago, Aldine, 1971.
————, *Biofeedback and Self-Control: An Aldine Annual on the Regulation of Bodily Processes and Consciousness.* Chicago, Aldine, published annually since 1970.
Jonas, Gerald, *Visceral Learning.* New York, Viking, 1973.